I0751956

Floral Treasures II

Thomas Roth Jr.

Floral Treasures II

Missing Toe Publishing
Chester South Carolina USA

Locations

The Photographs in the following pages were created in three different locations. Glen Carin Gardens in Rock Hill South Carolina, Daniel Stowe Botanical Garden in Gastonia North Carolina, and my front yard garden in Chester South Carolina.

I have listed the names of the flowers using common names. Some flowers have several different names and, I have used the one I have heard the most.

The photographs on the following pages were created between 2010 and 2012.

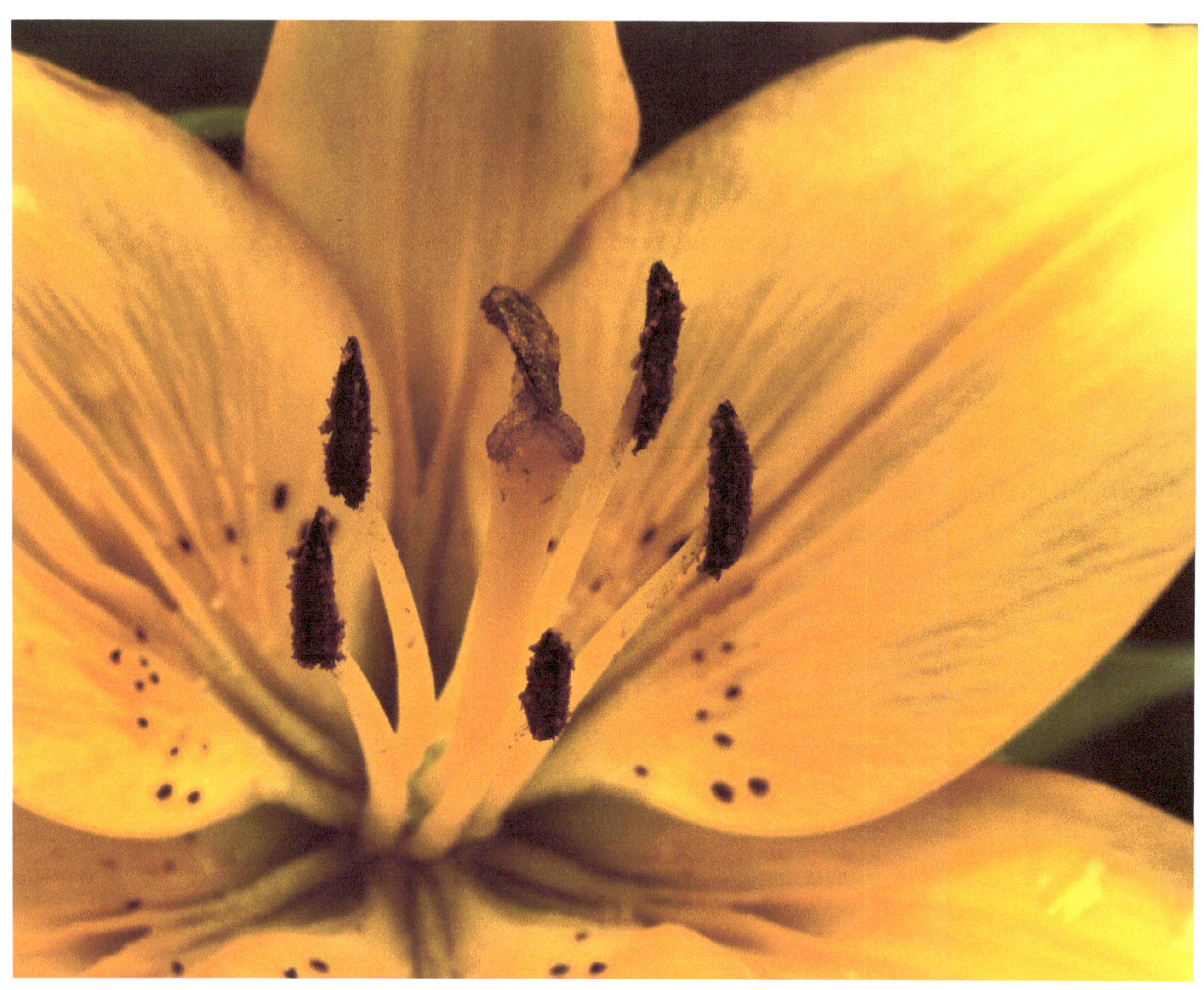

Peach Color Asiatic Lilly

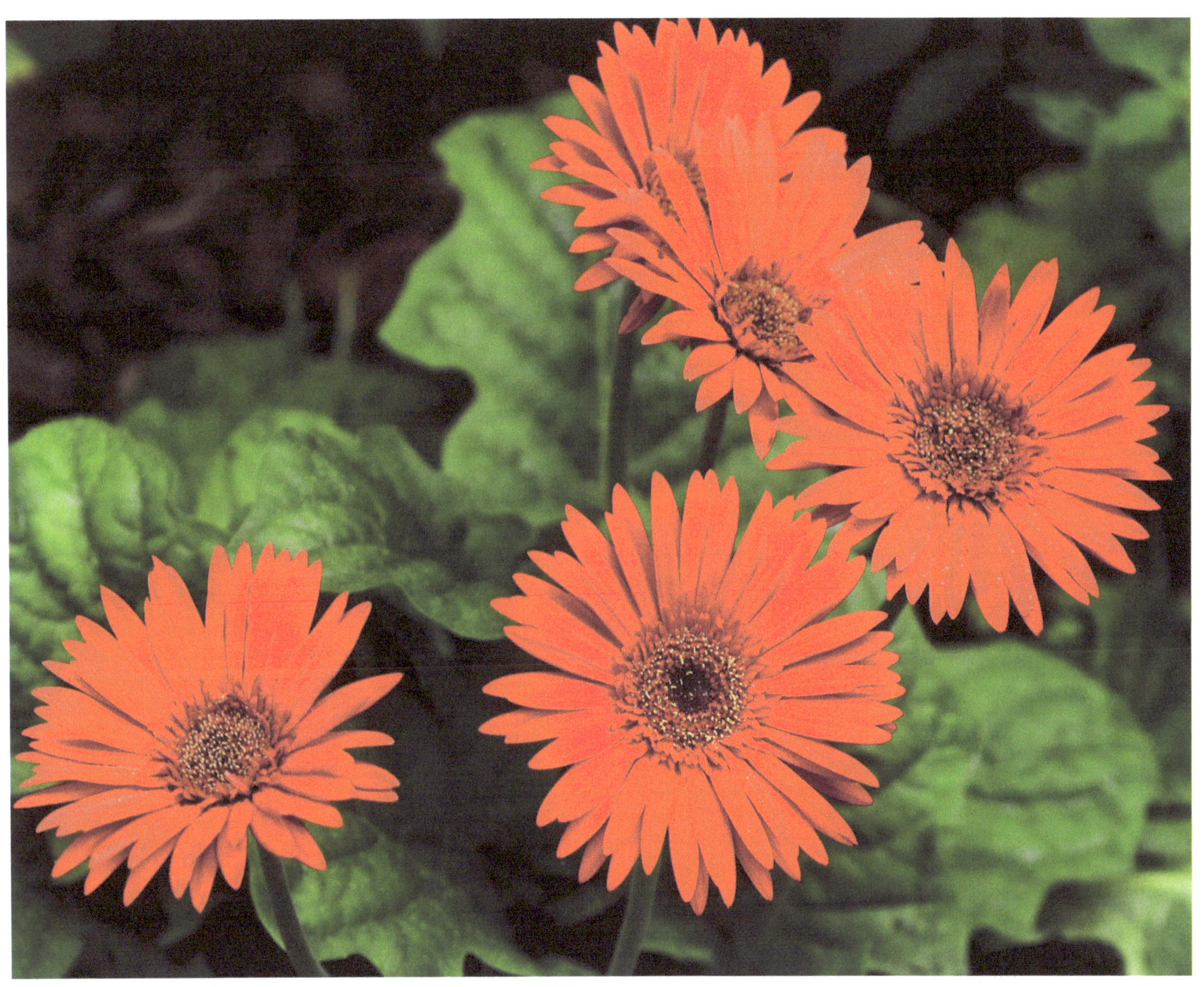

Red Gerbera Daisy

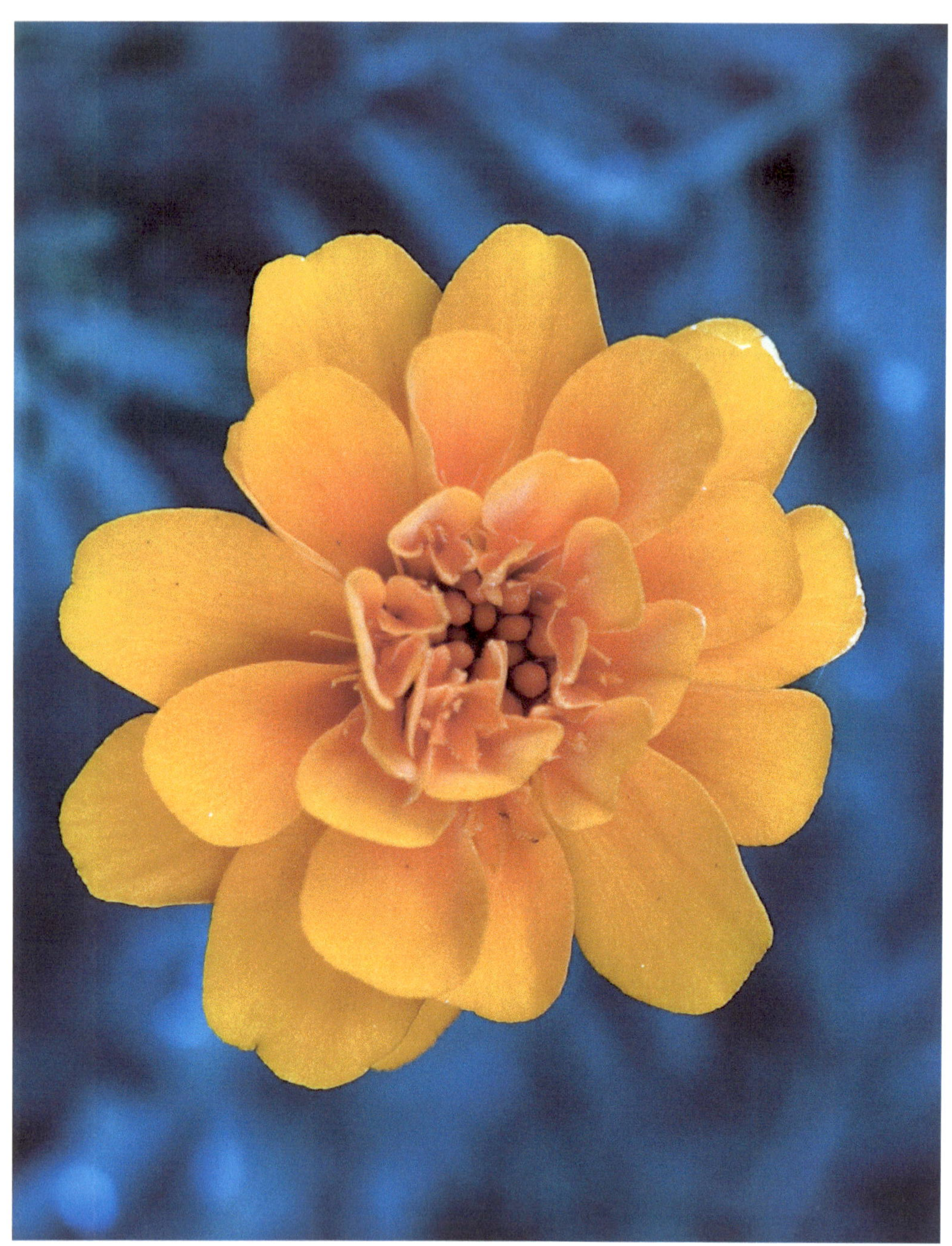

Merrigold

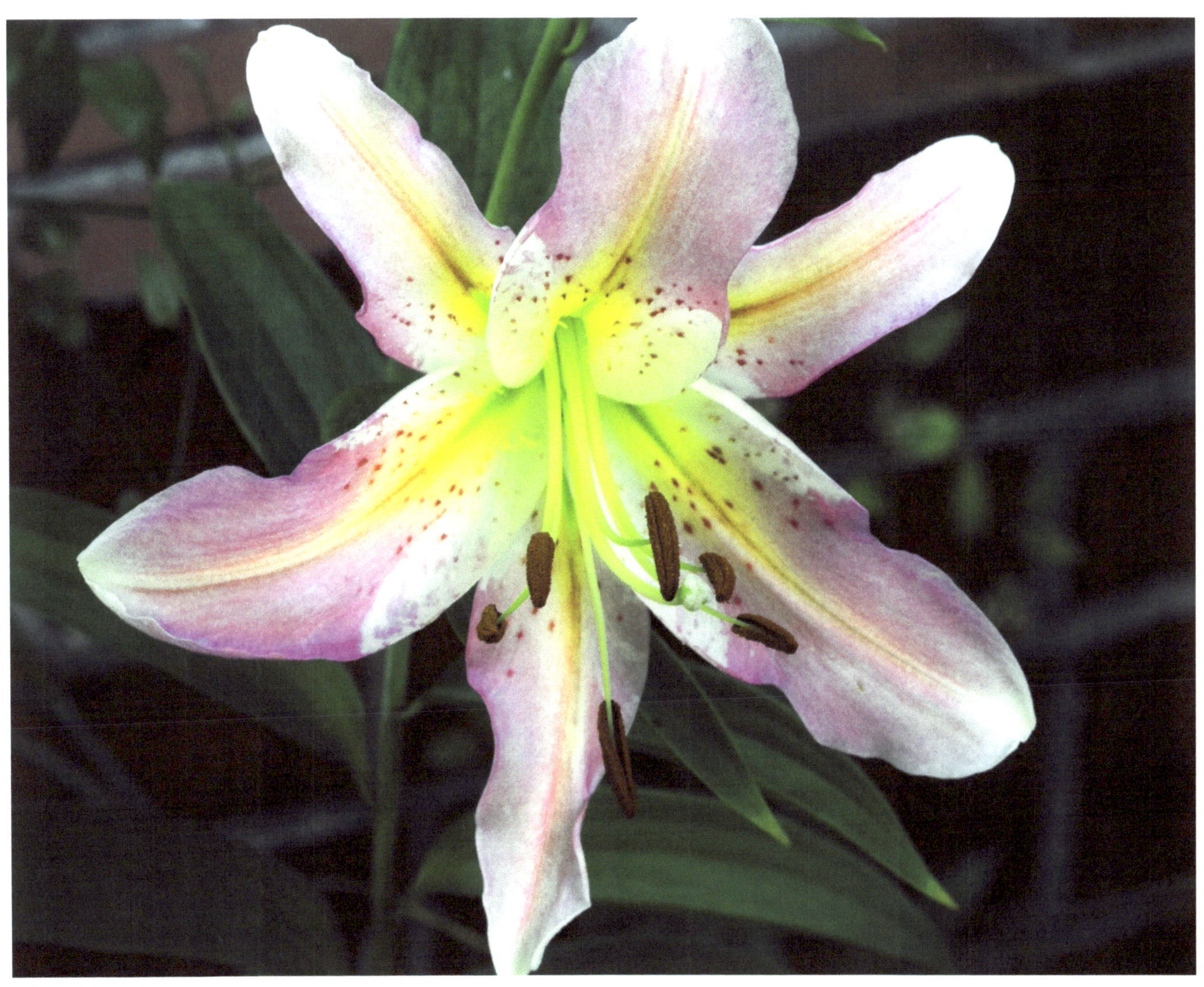

Pink Orientinal Lilly   (Le Reve)

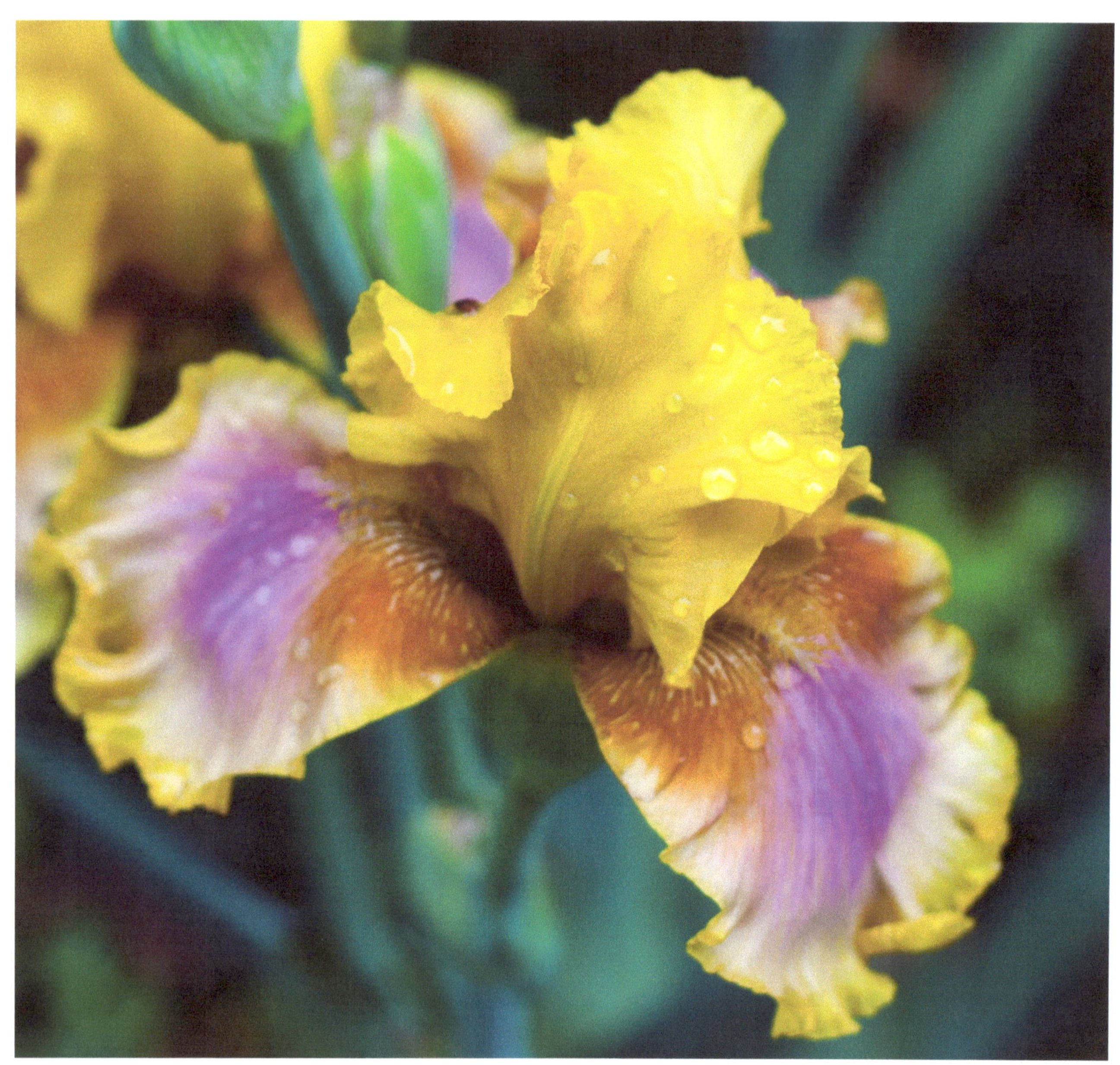

Yellow and Lavender Iris

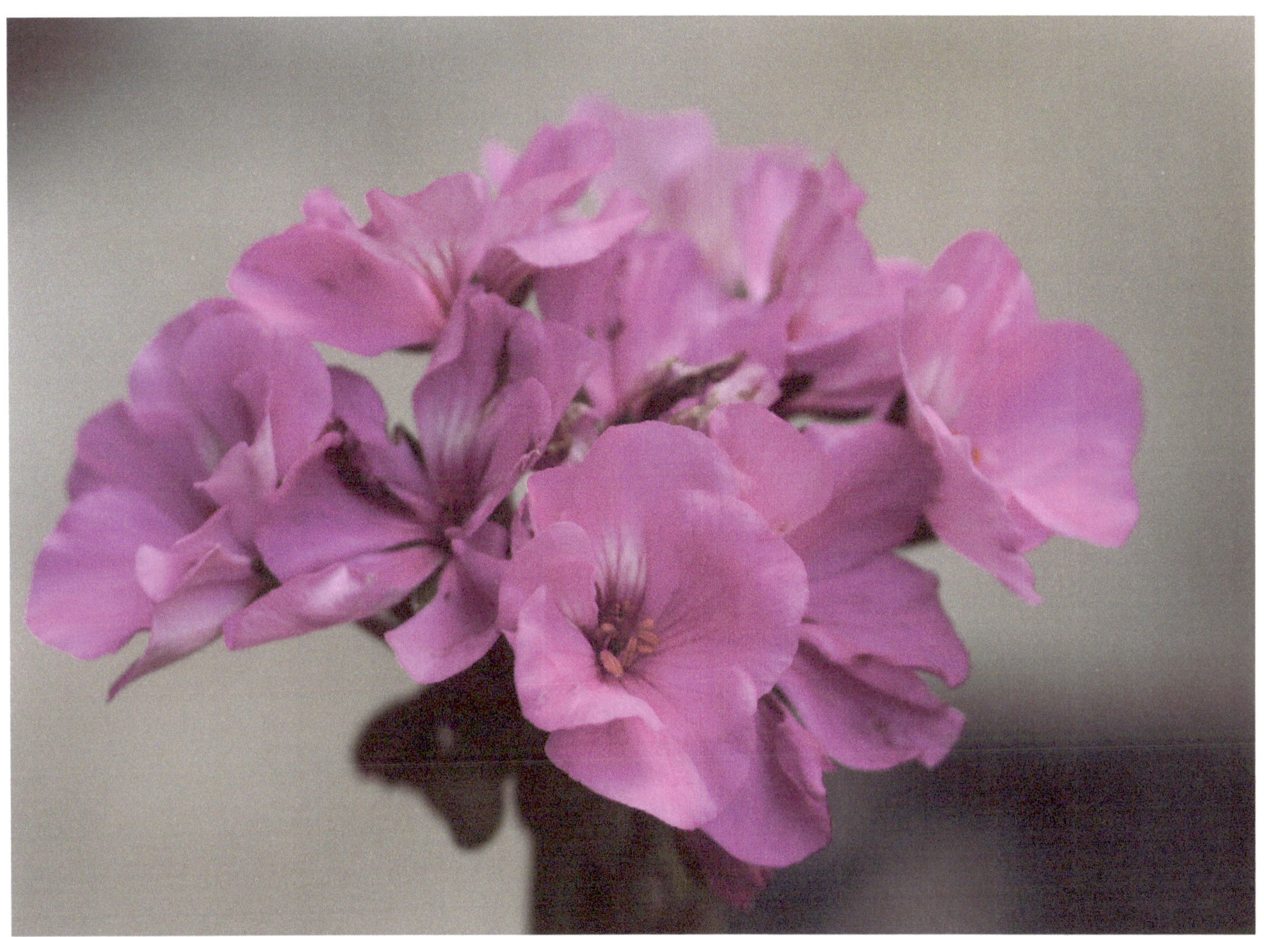

Summer Phlox

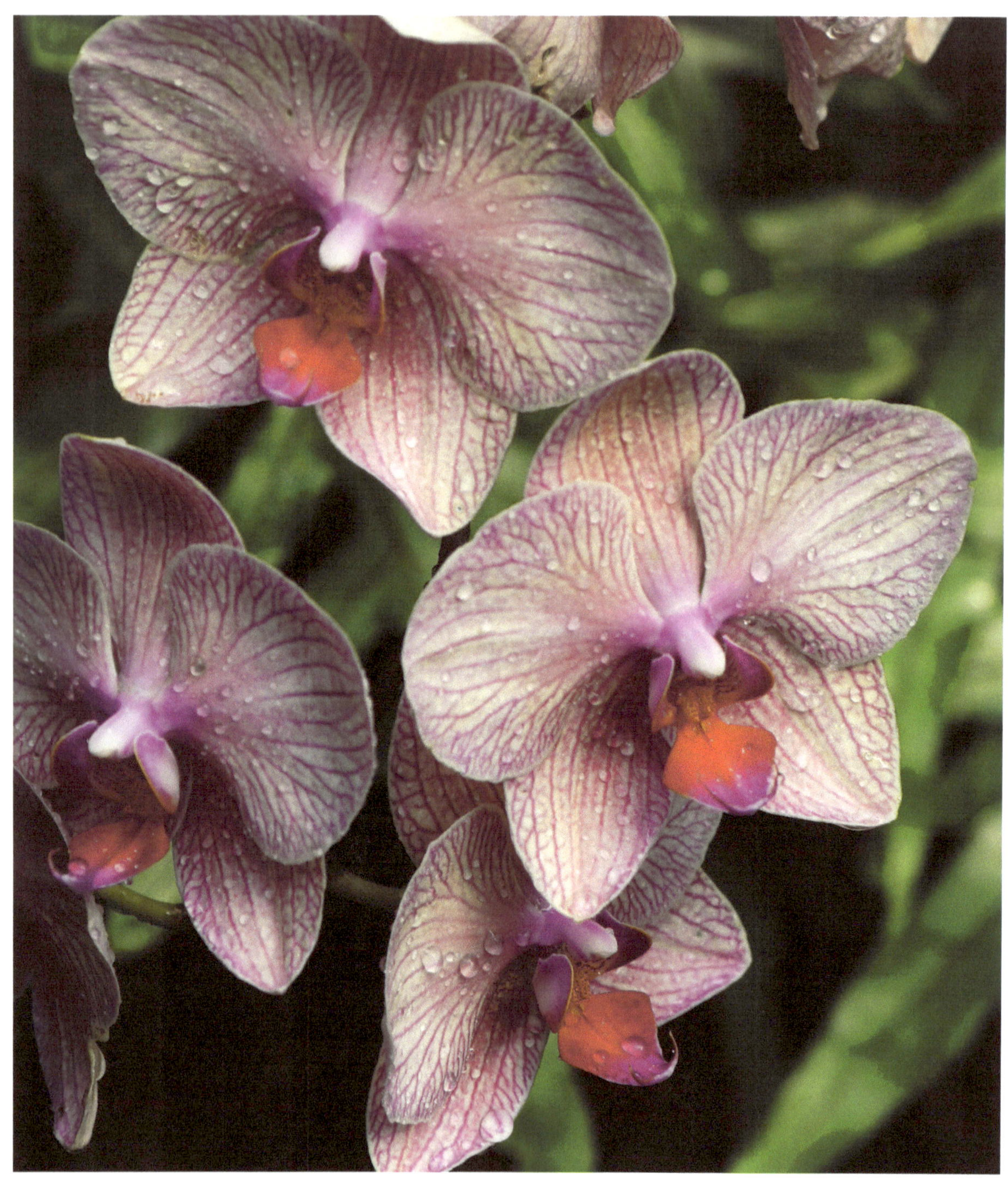

Phalaenopsis Orchid

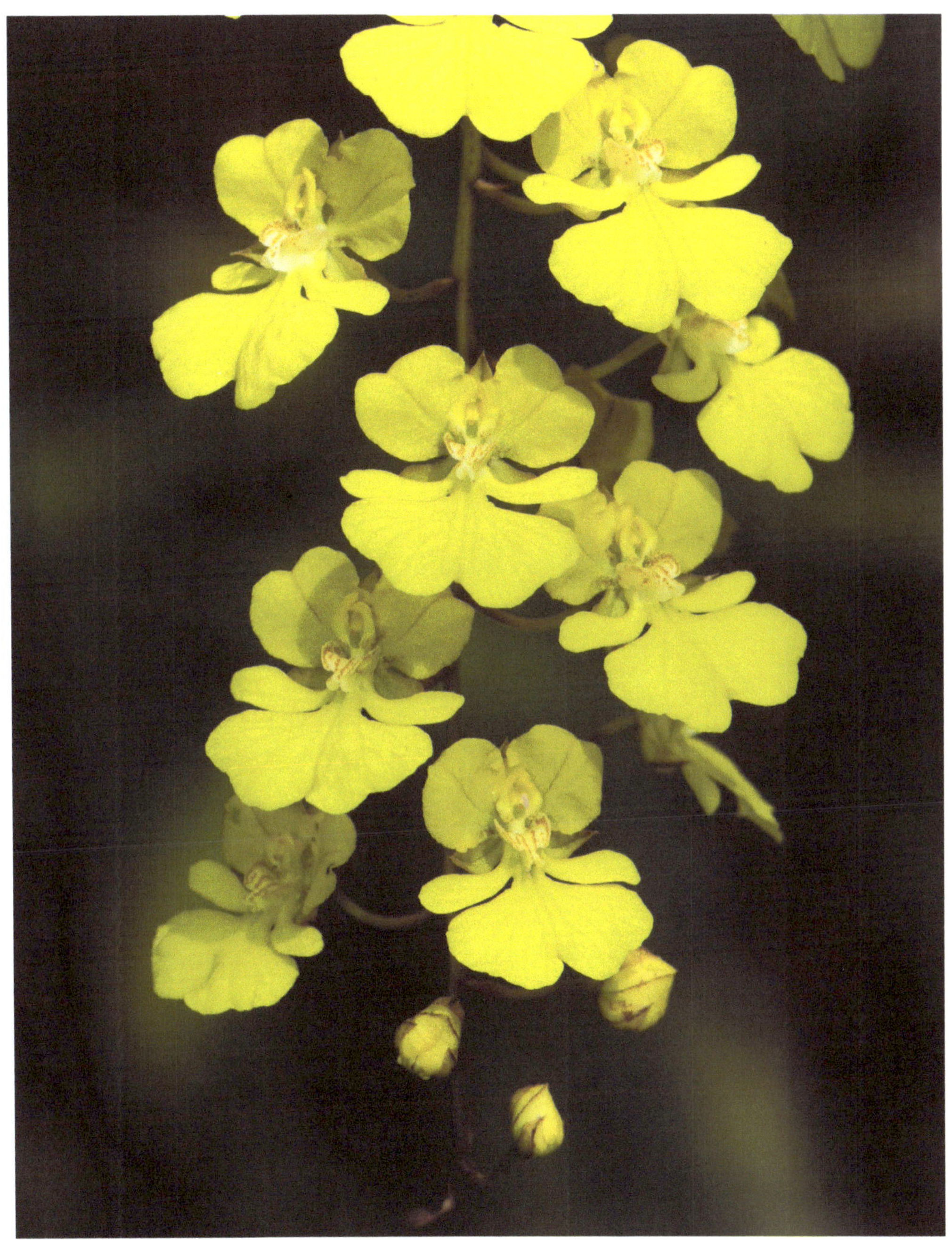

Oncidium Orchids

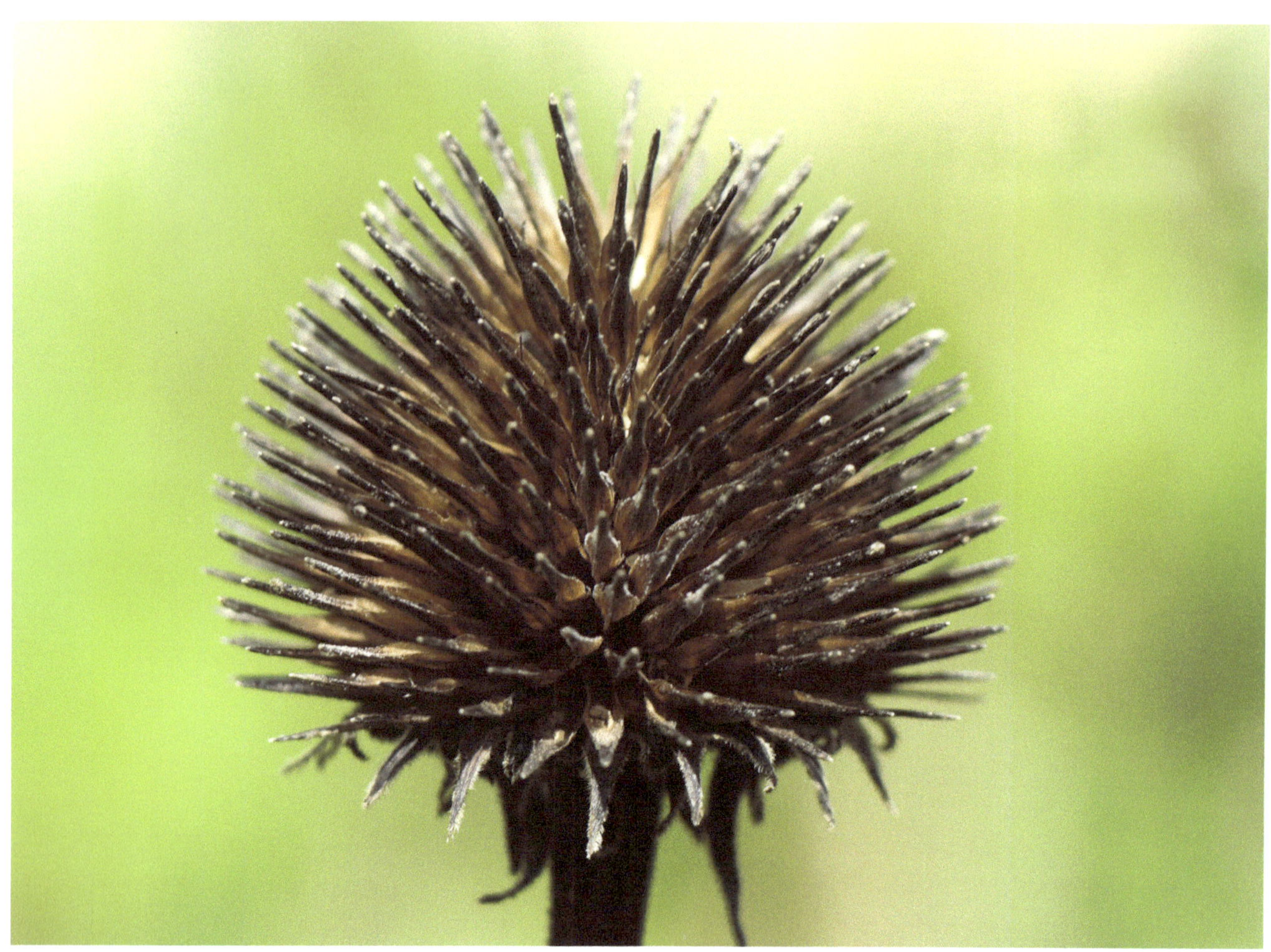

Thistle

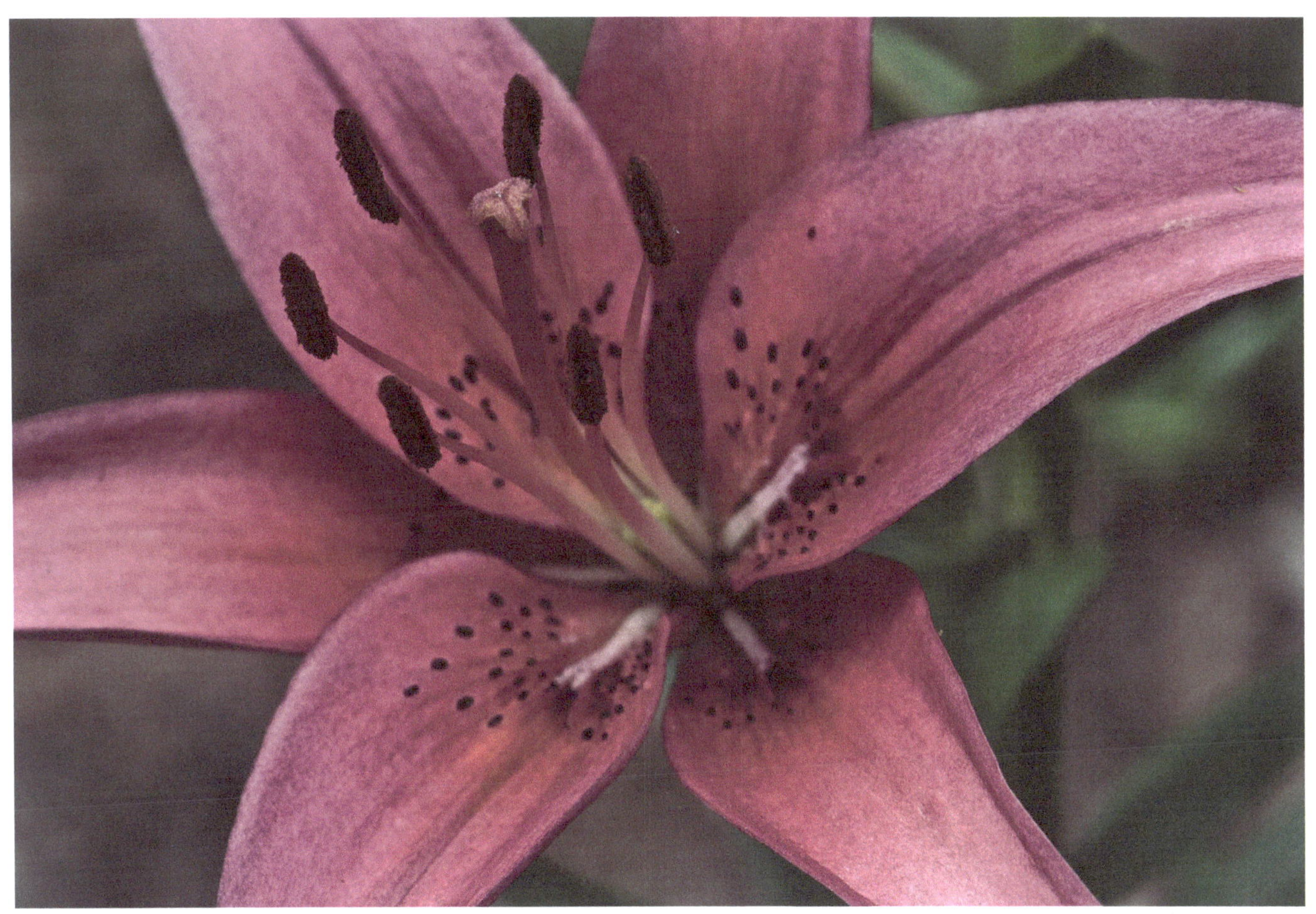

Hot Pink Asiatic Lilly

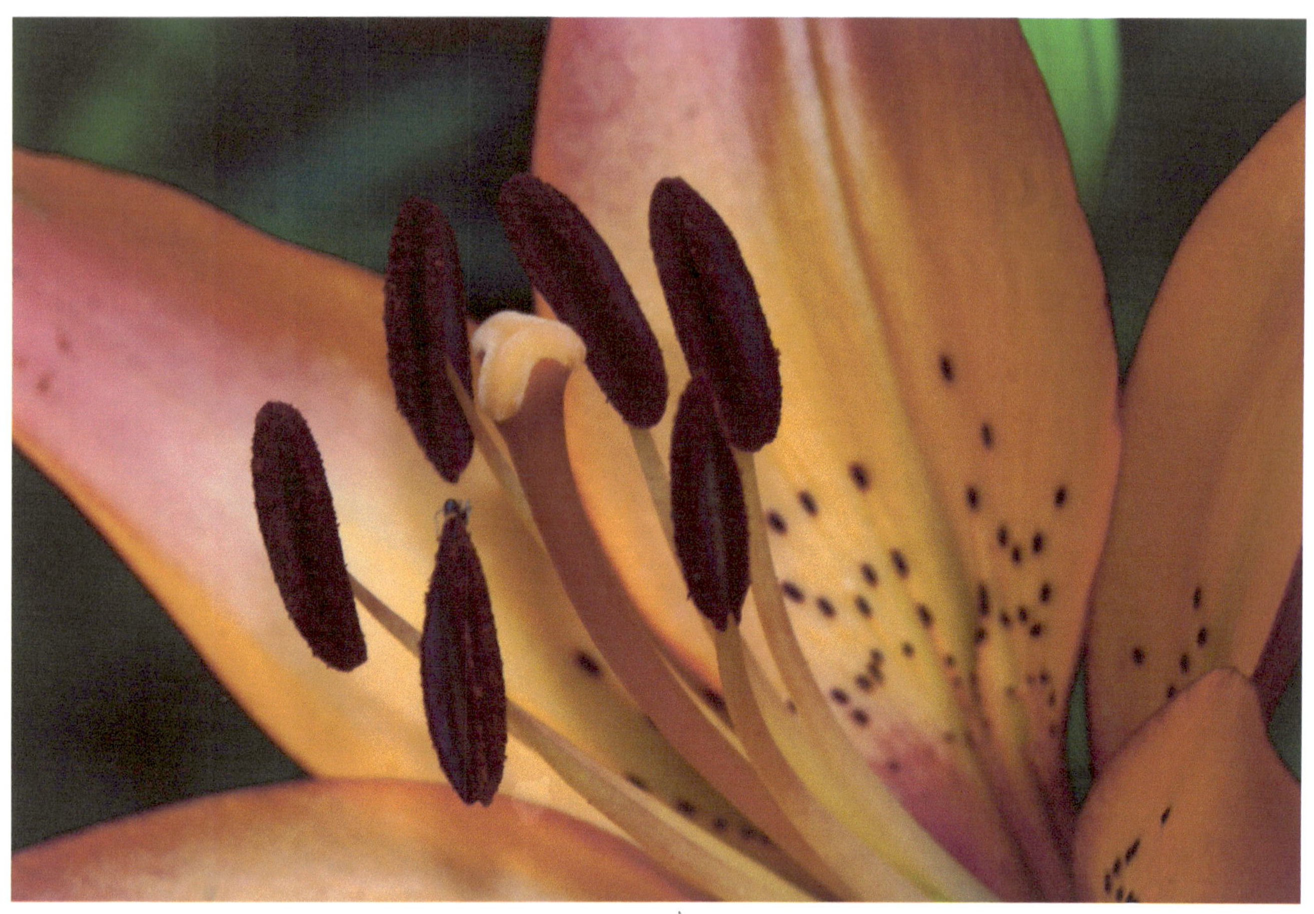

Close up of a Peach Colored Asiatic Lilly

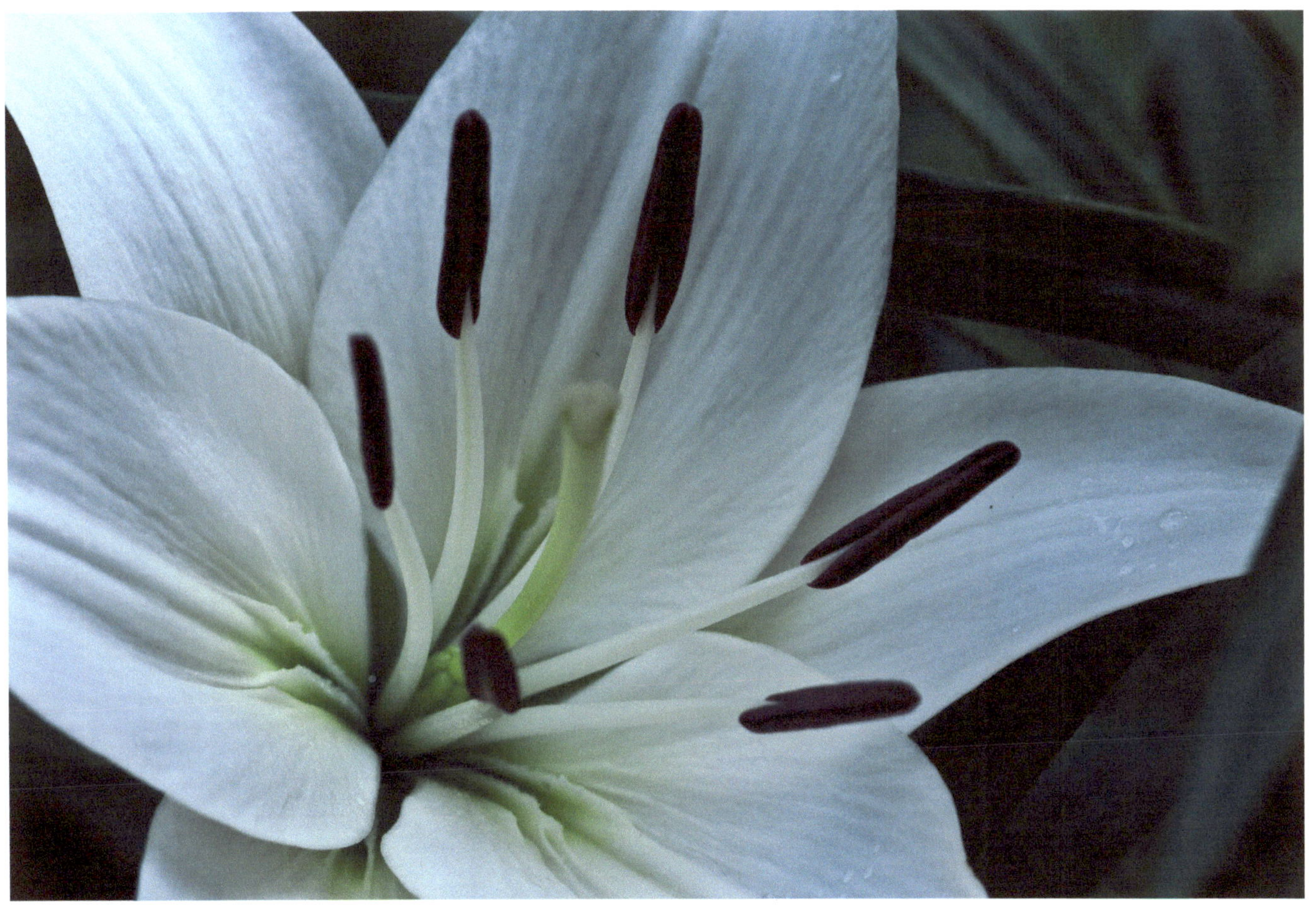

White Asiatic Lilly

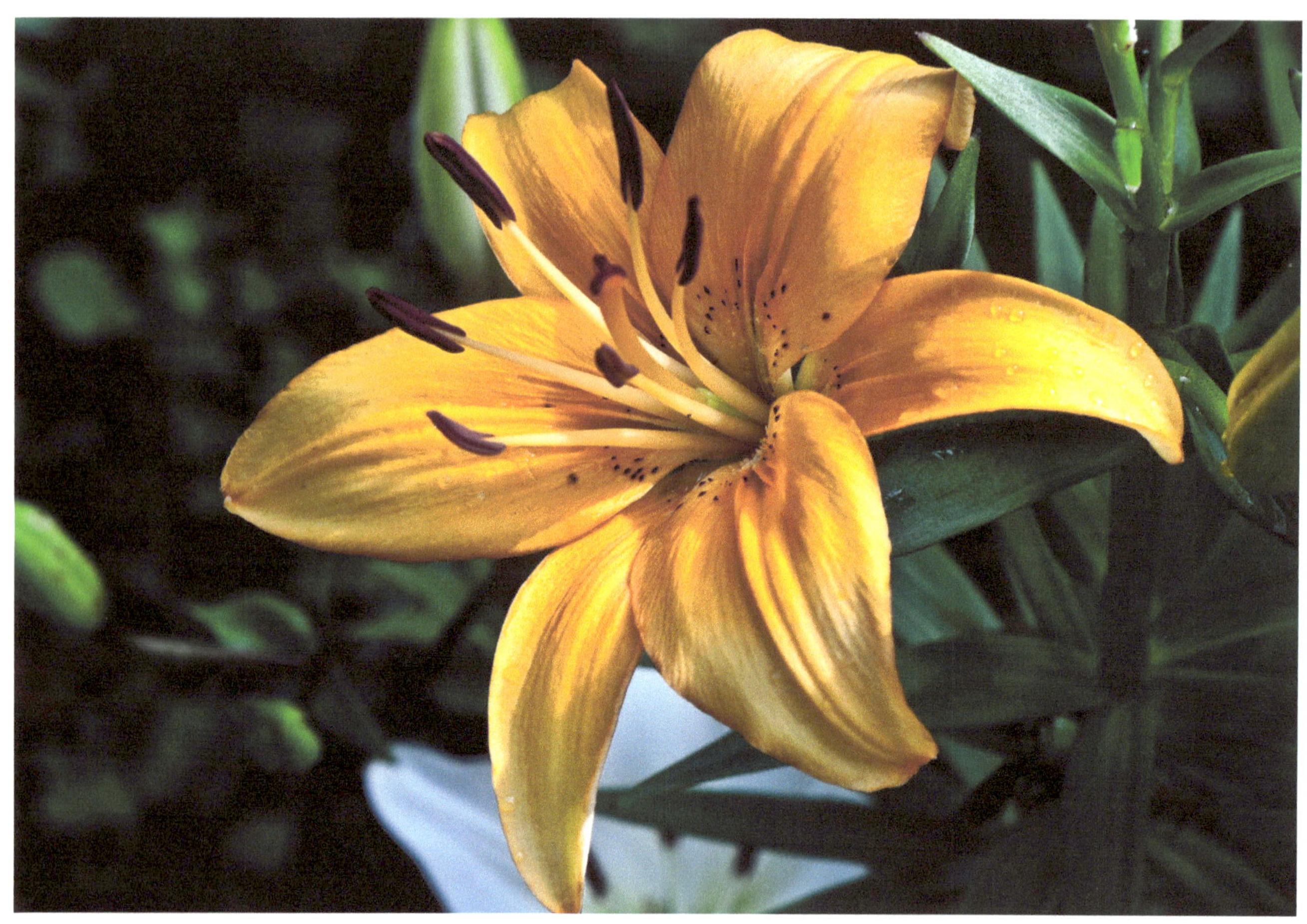

Peach Asiatic Lilly in Full Sun

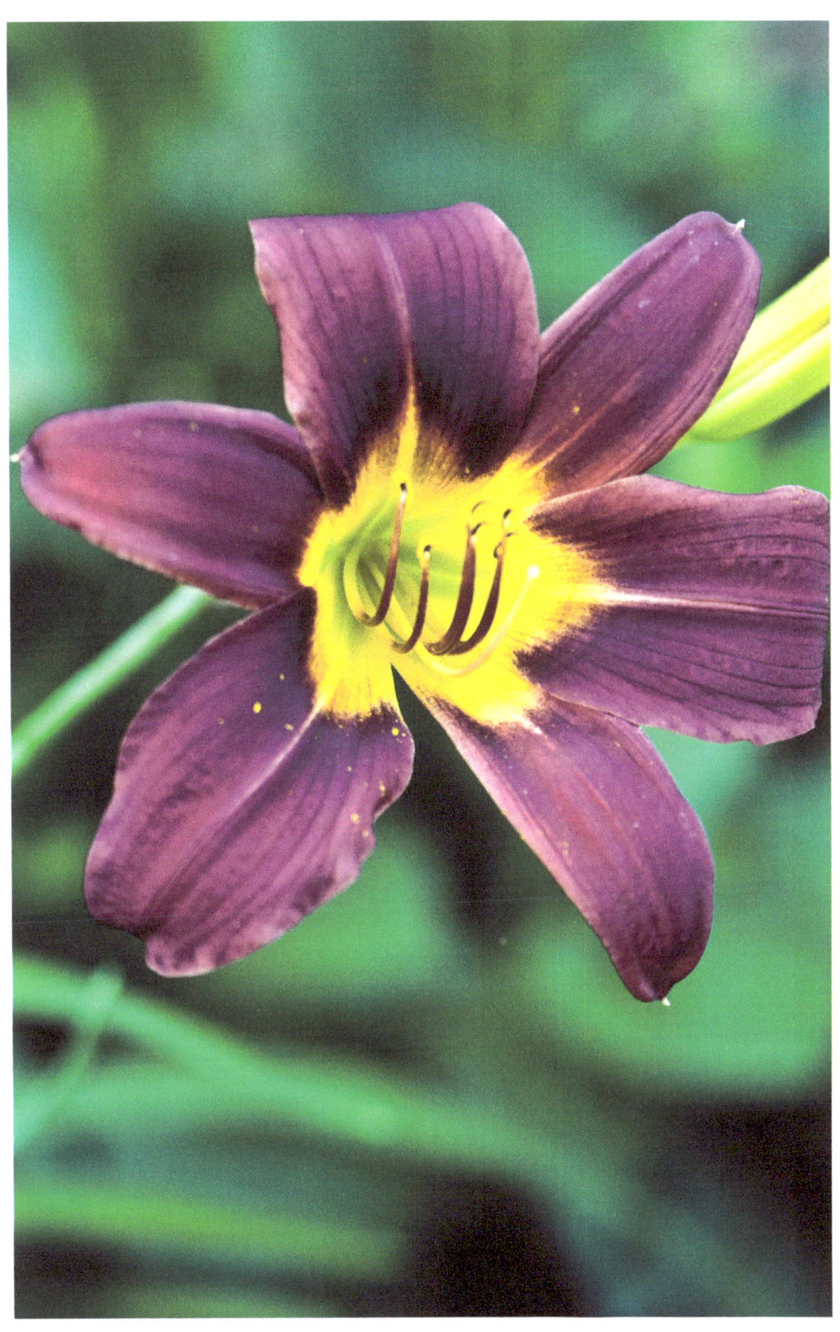

Purple Day Lilly

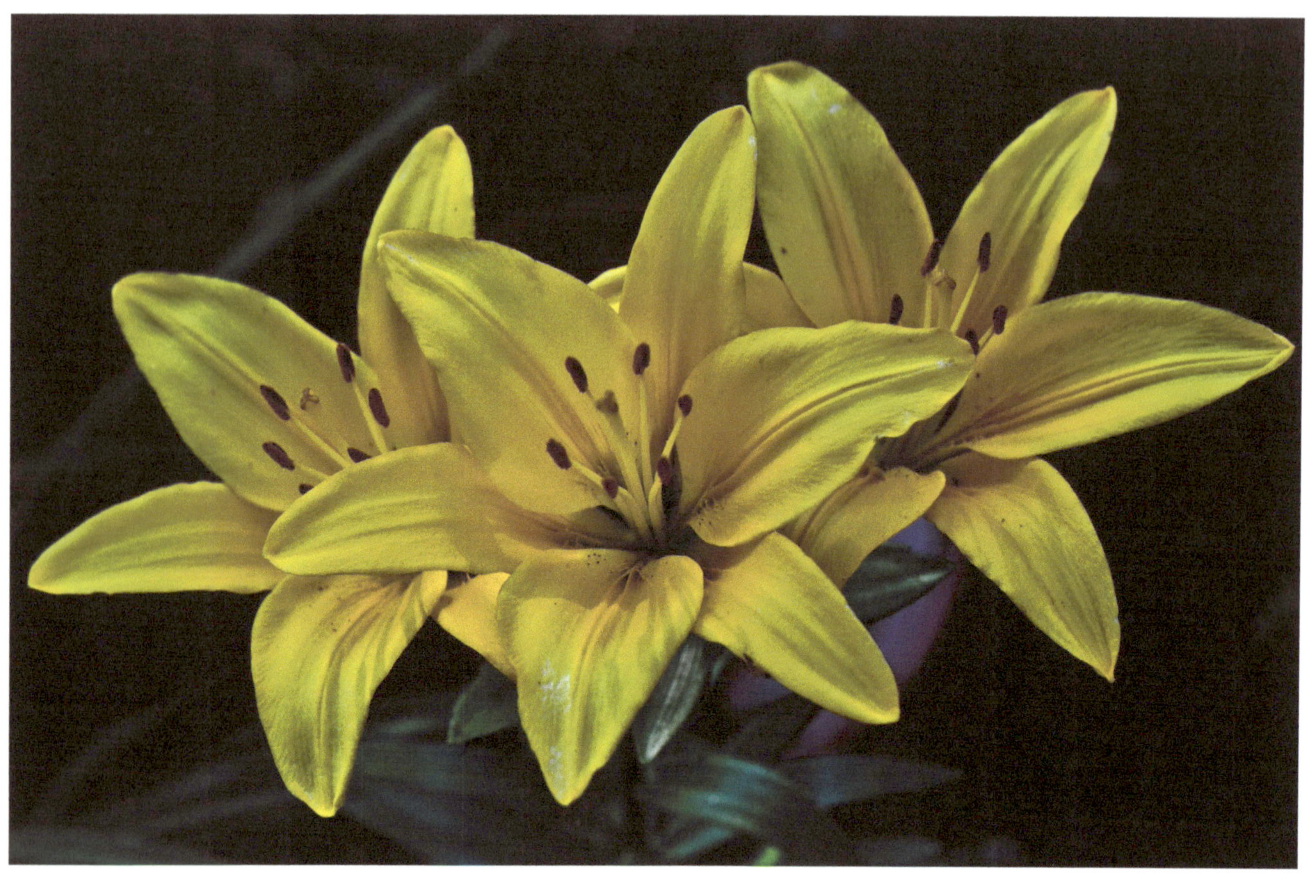

Yellow Asiatic lilly

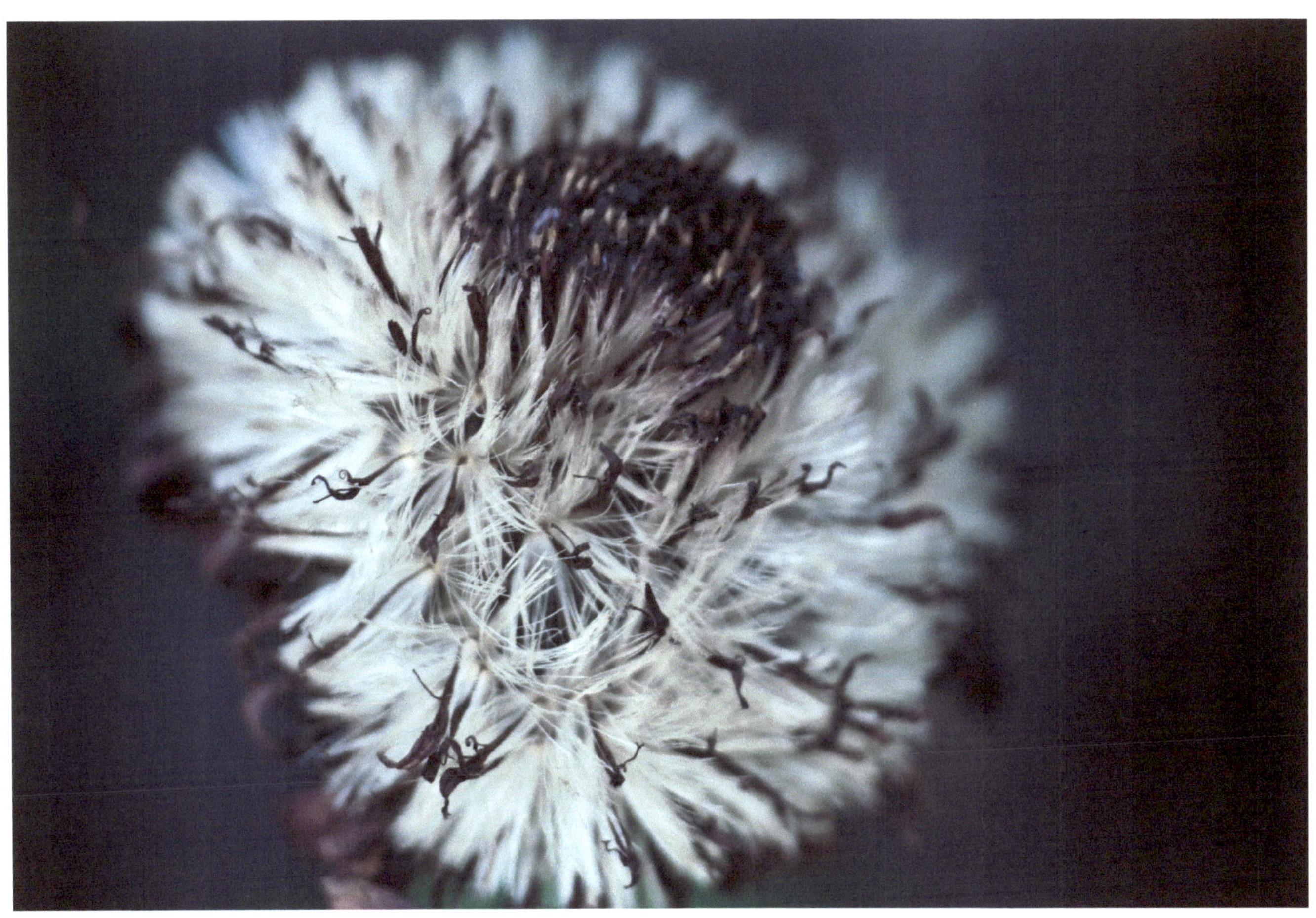

Black Eye Susan in early Winter

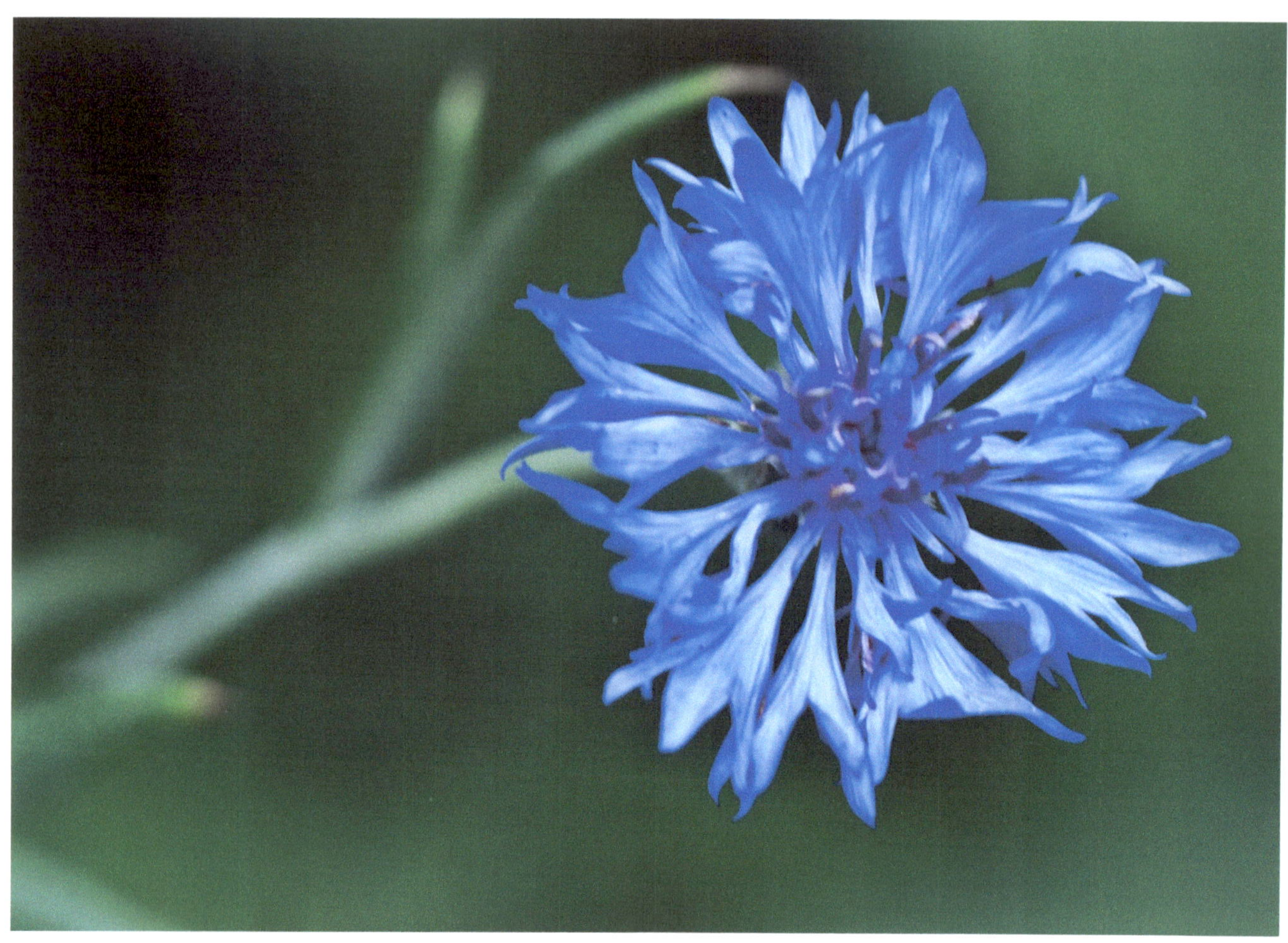

Blue Cornflower

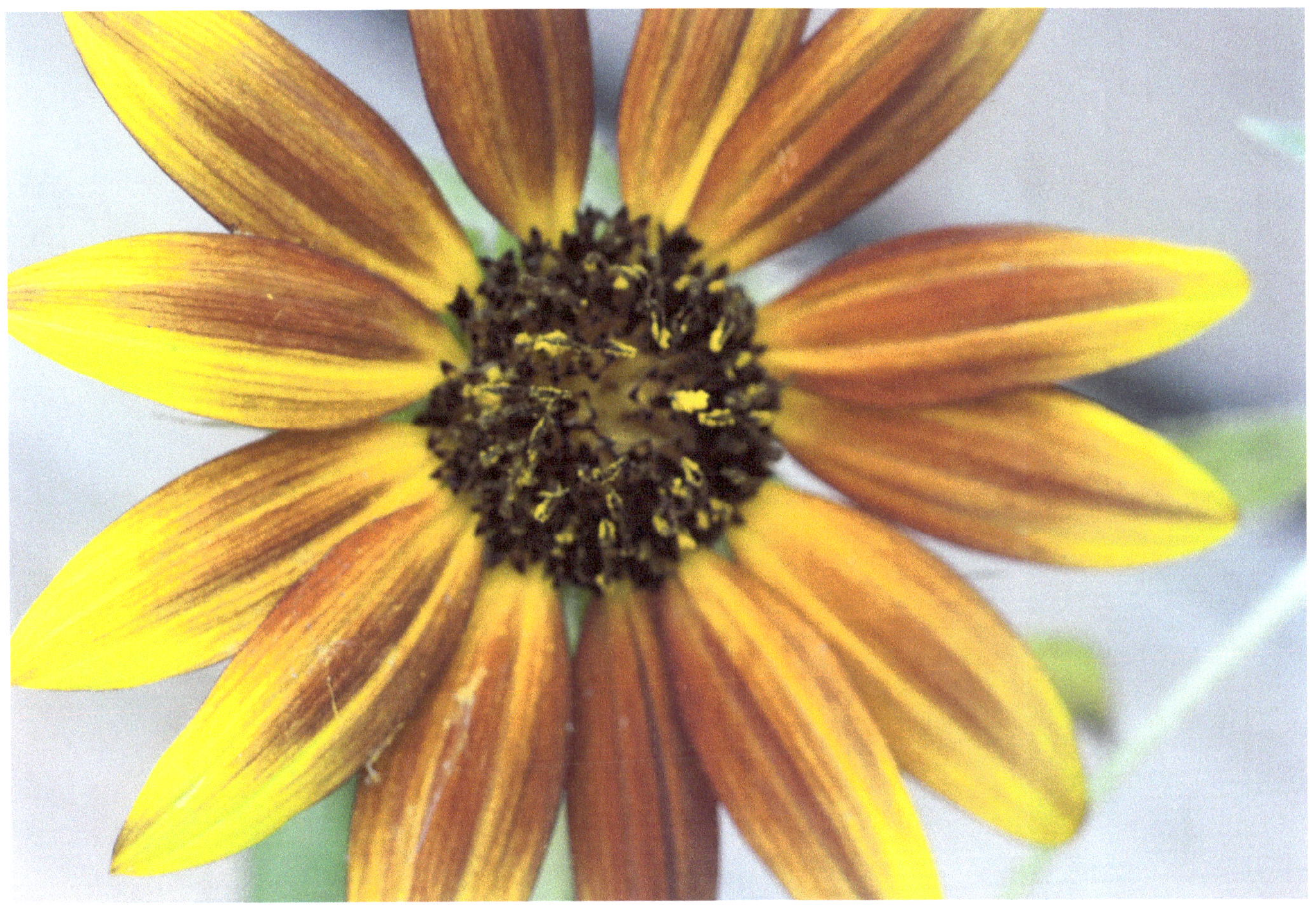

Bi-Color Sunflower

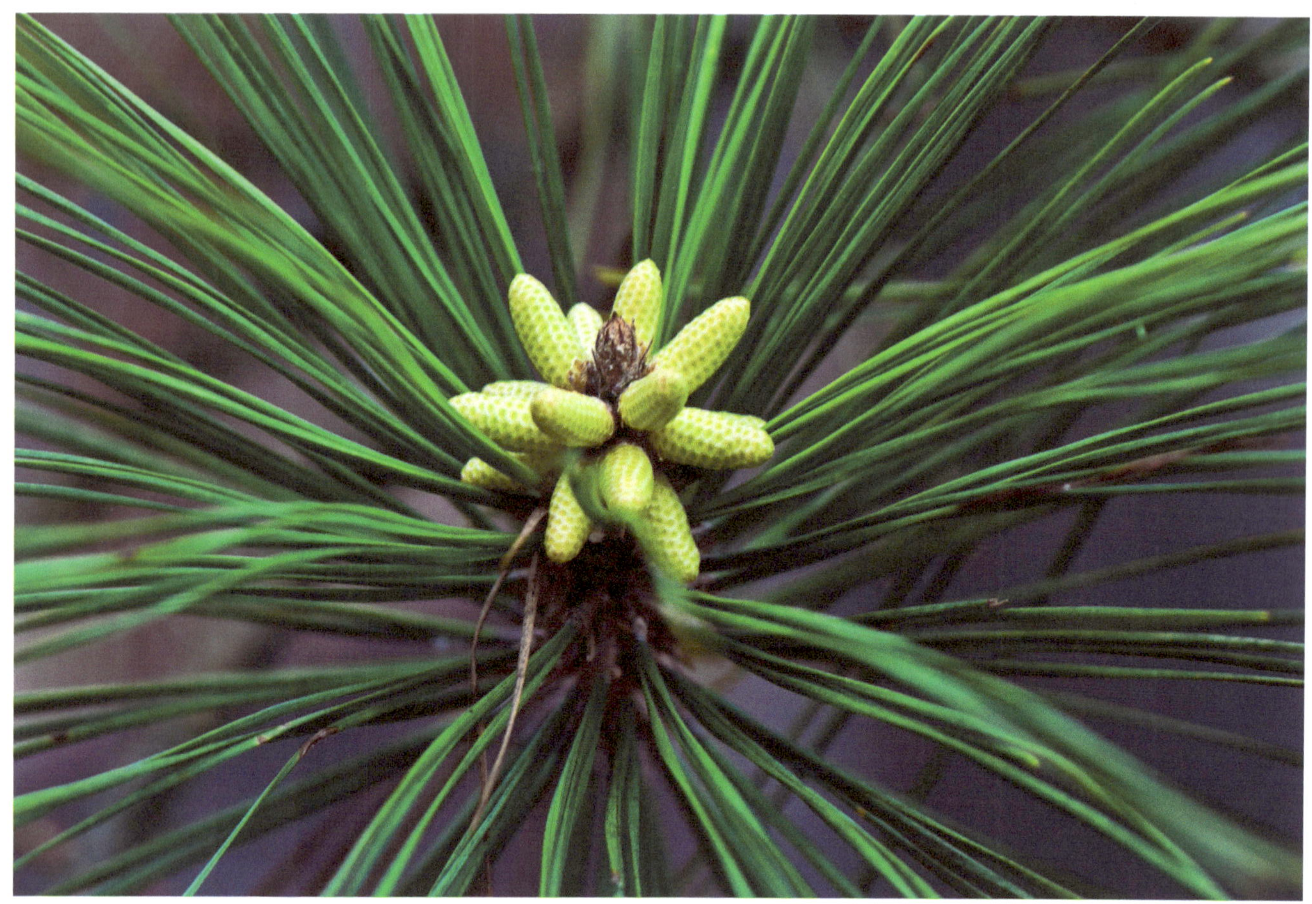

Baby Pine Cones

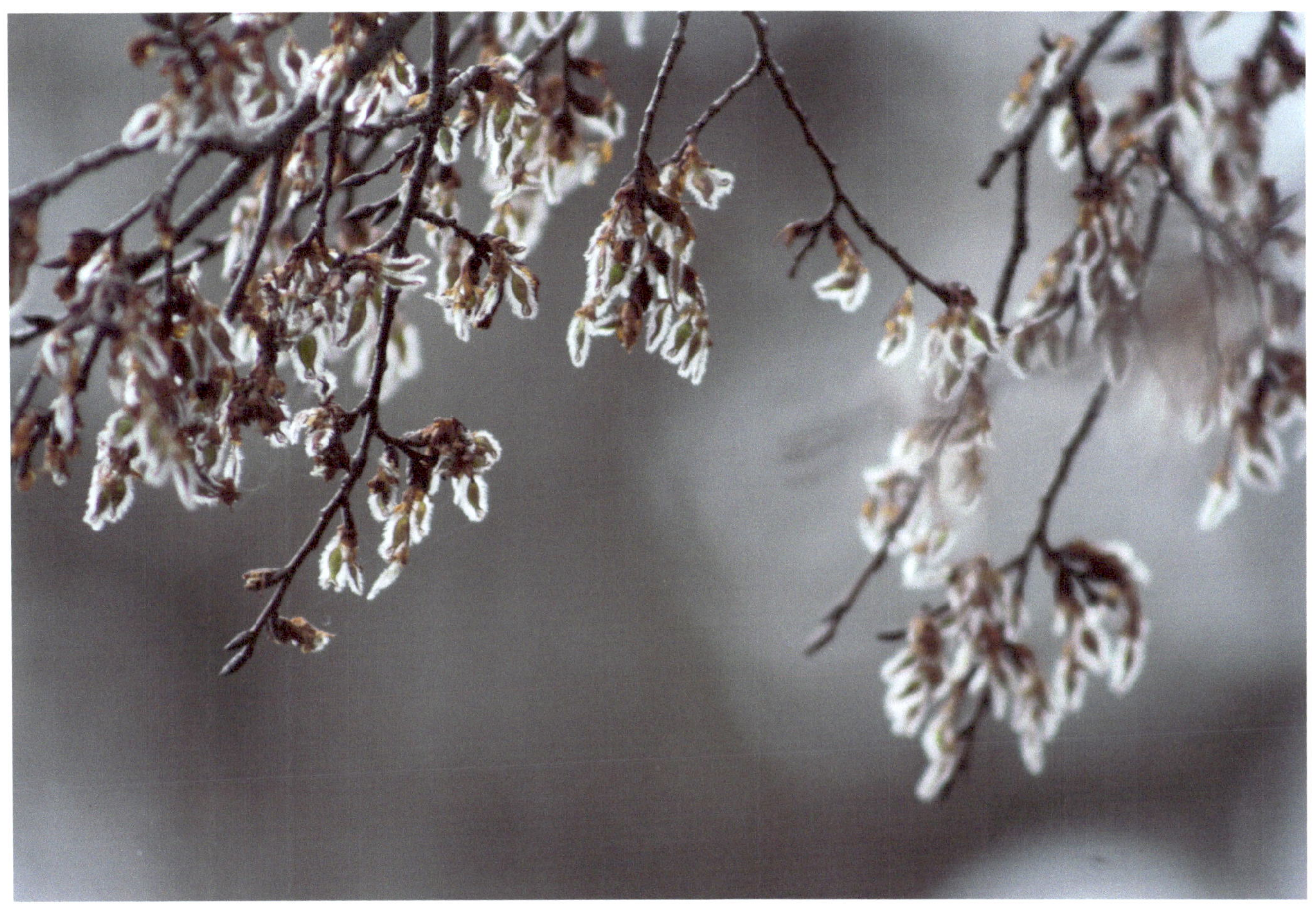

Tree Branches in the Fall

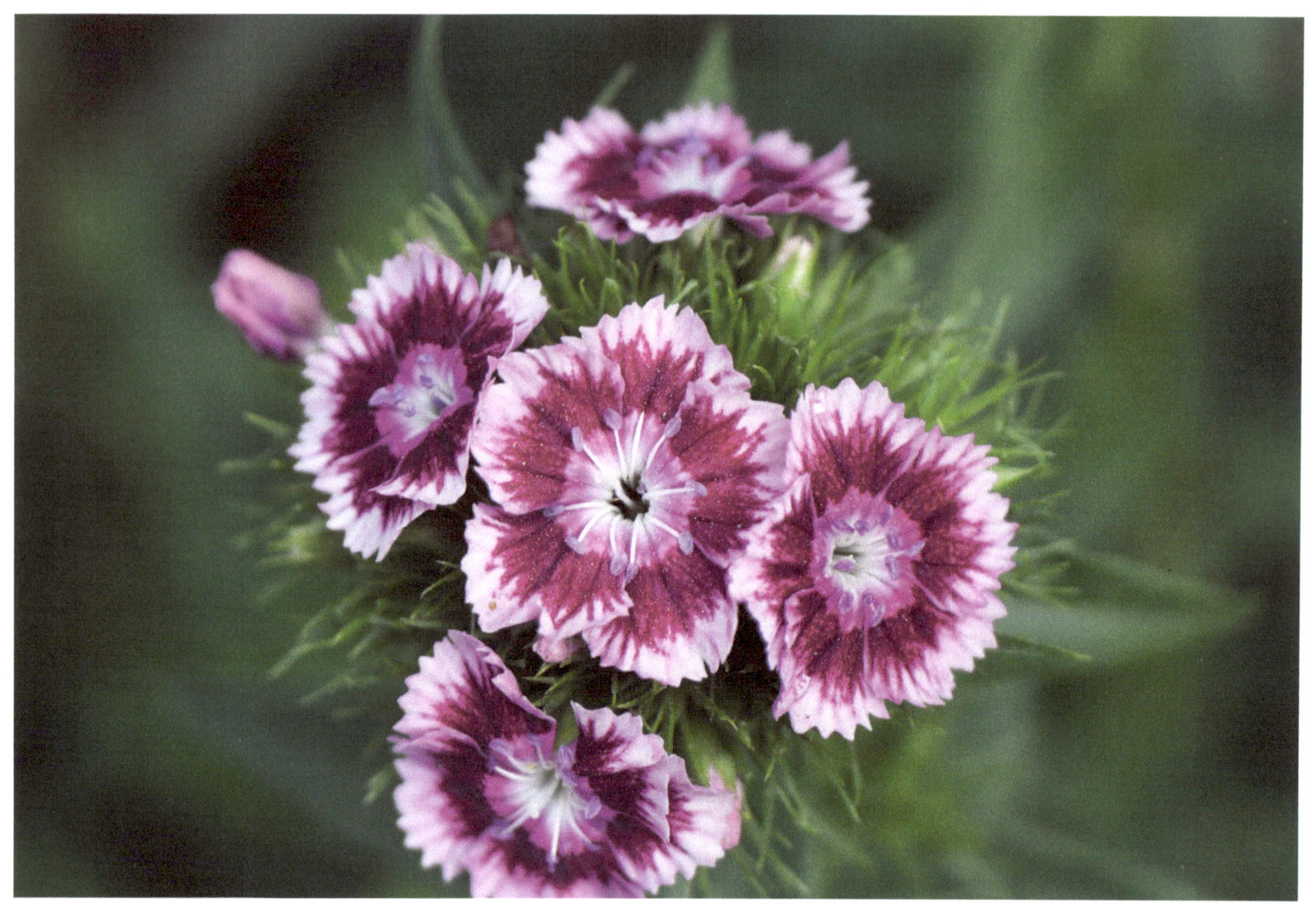

Sweet William

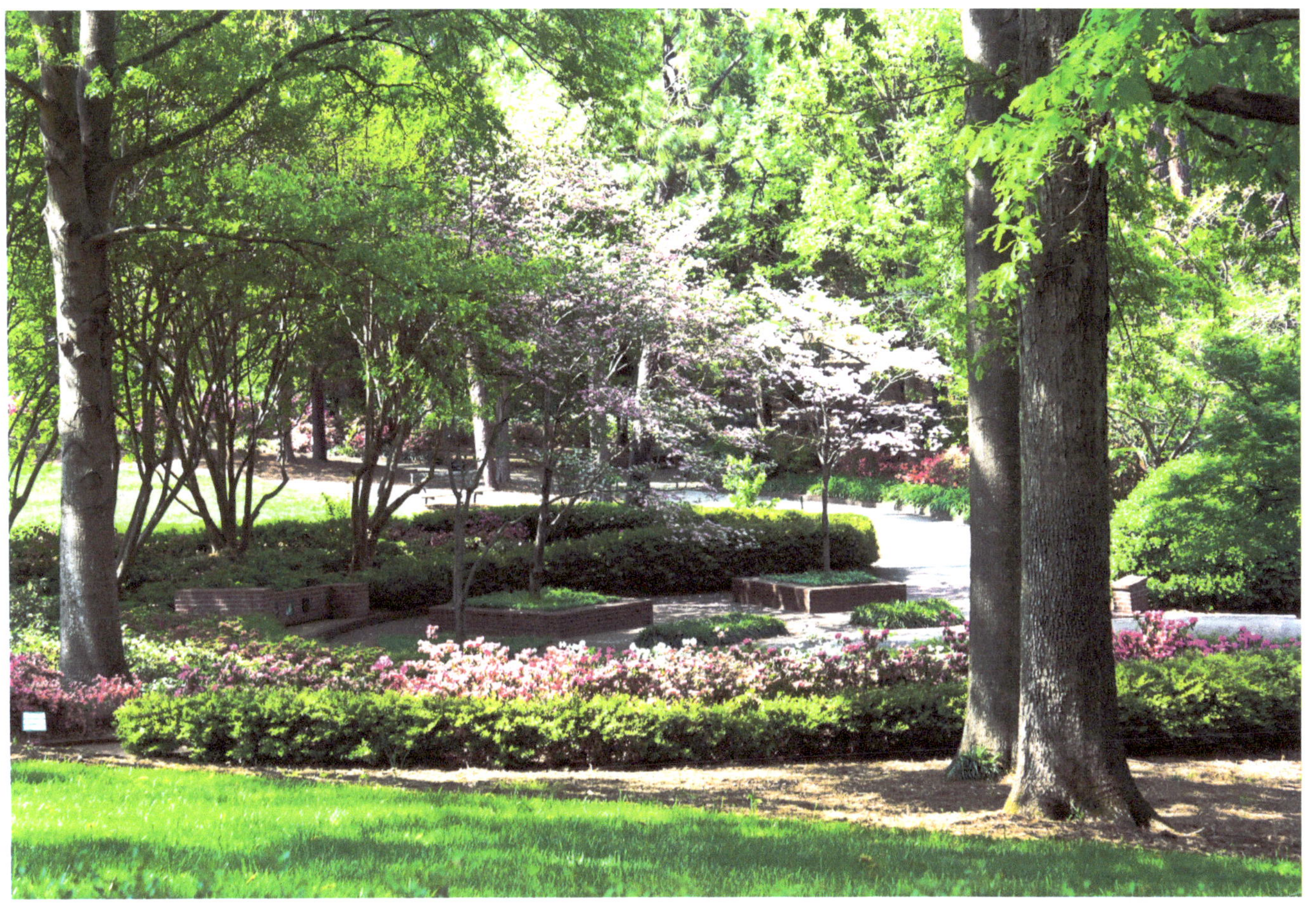

Glen Carin Garden in the Spring

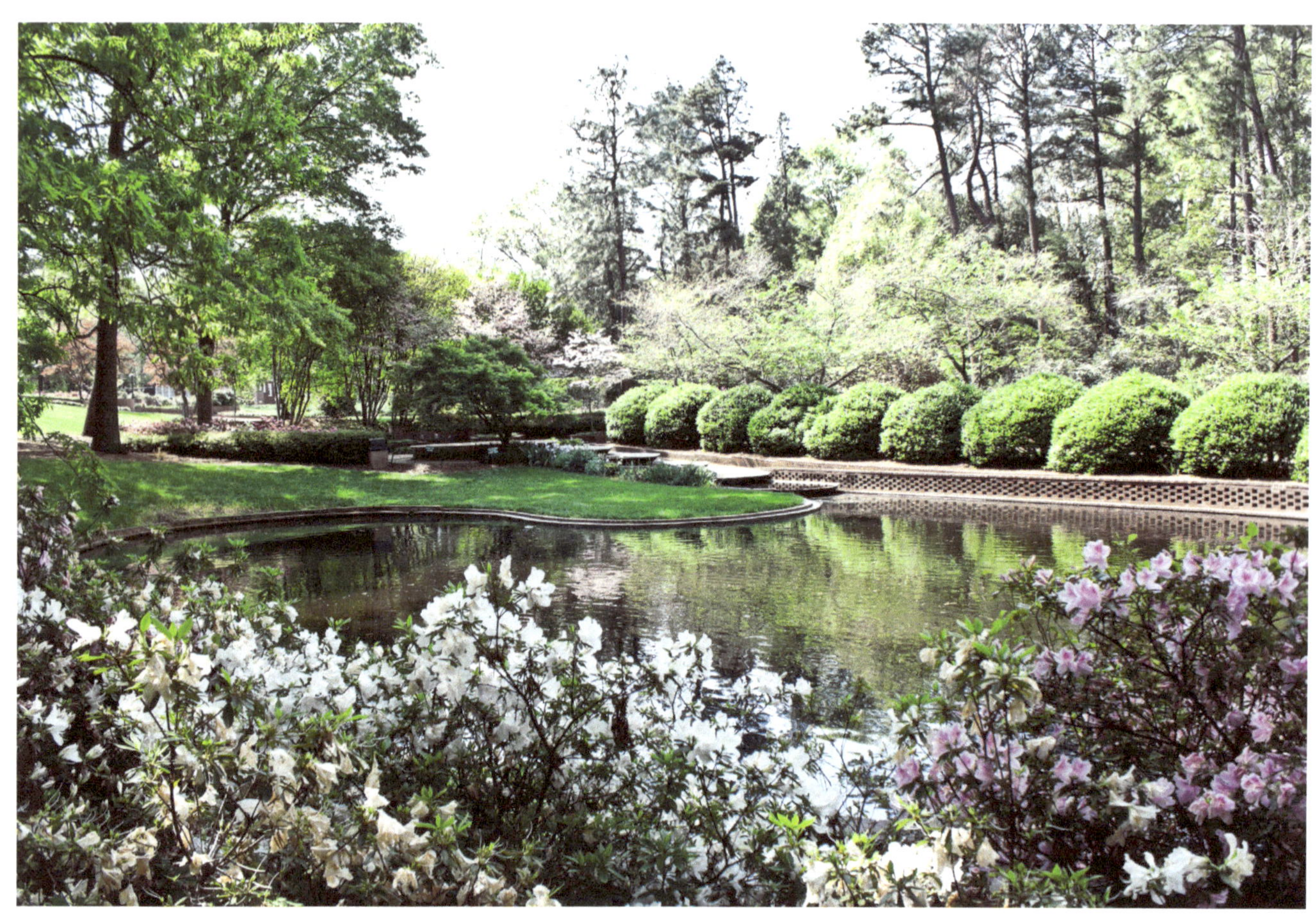

Glen Carin Garden in the Spring

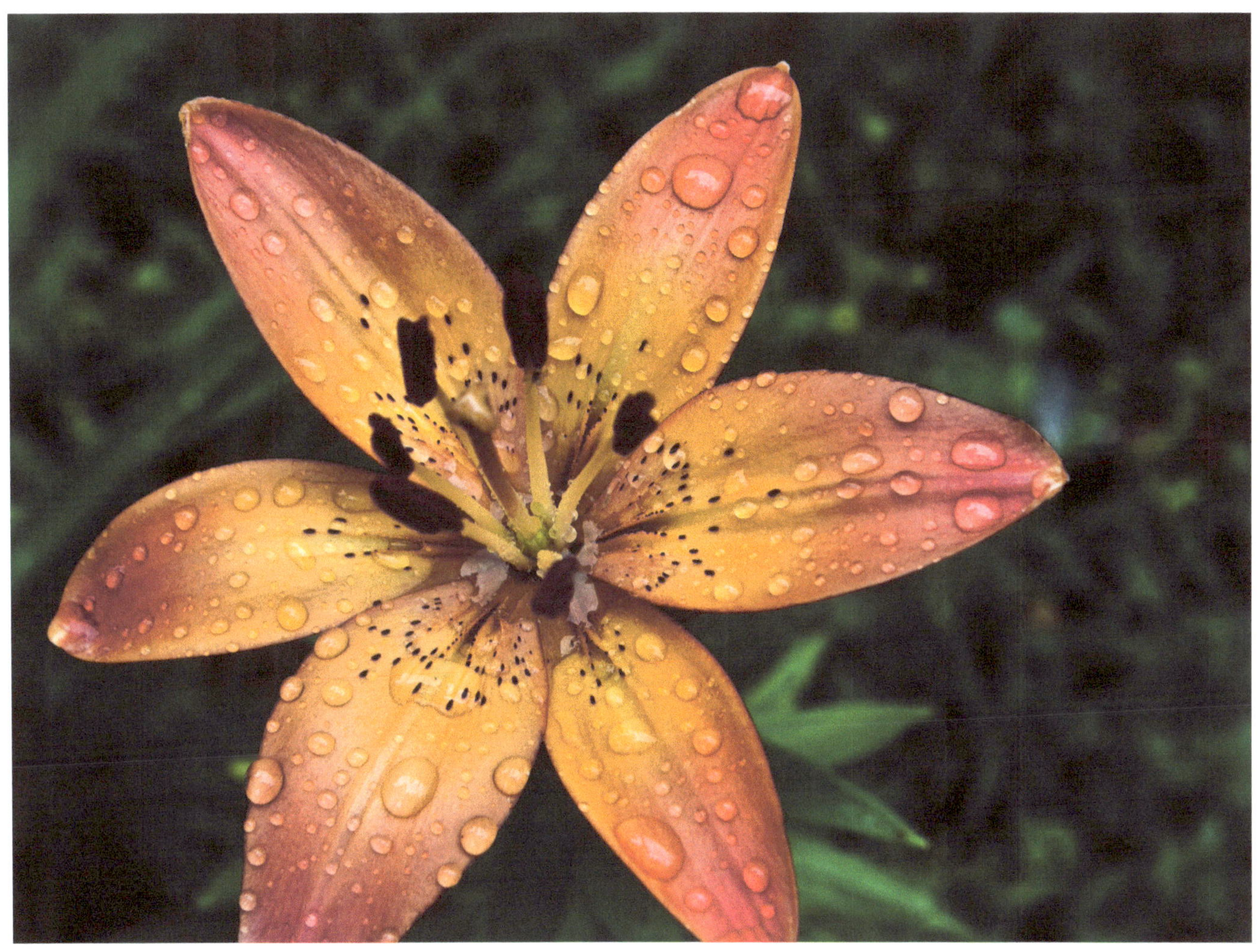

Asiatic Lilly in the Rain

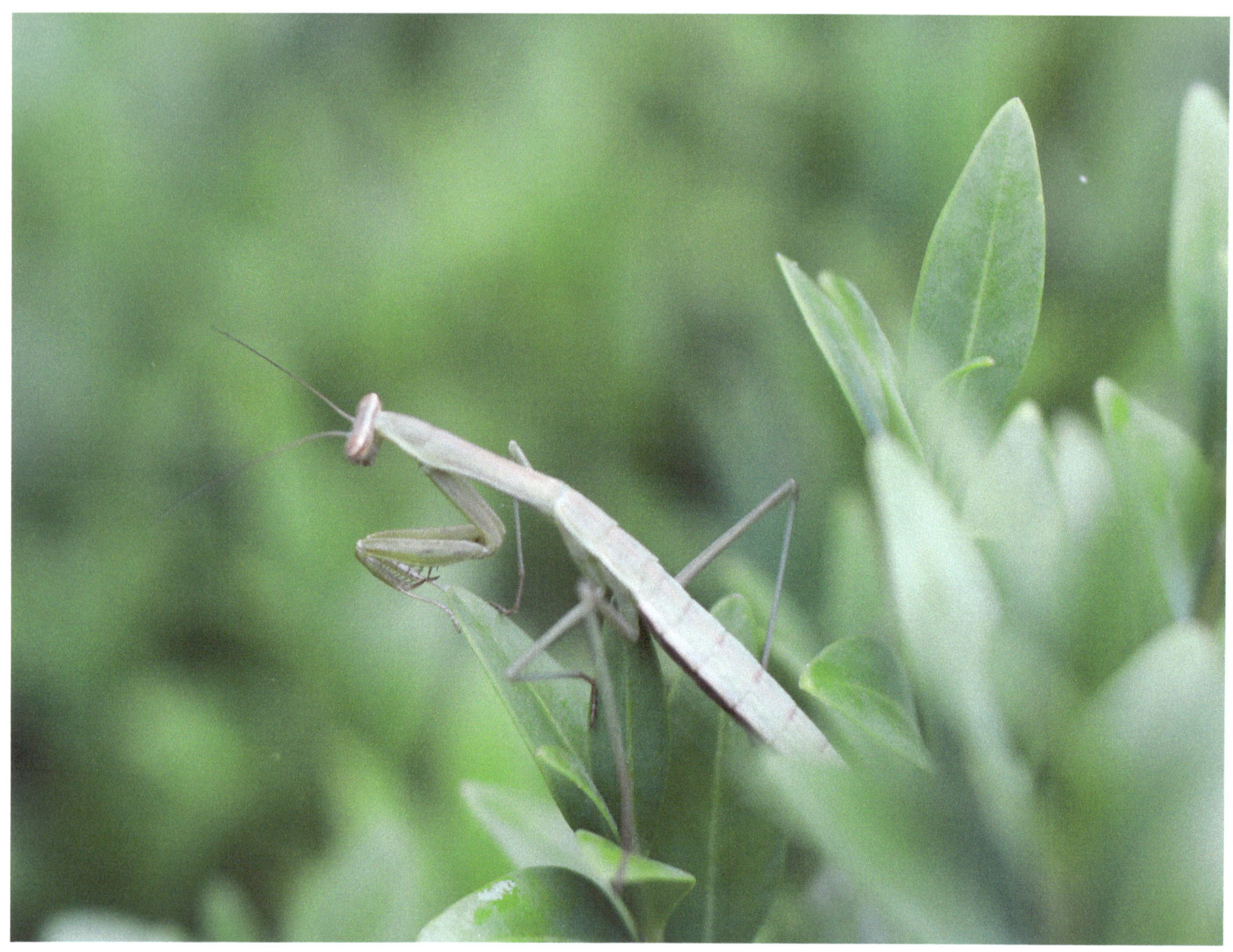

Praying Mantis in the Garden

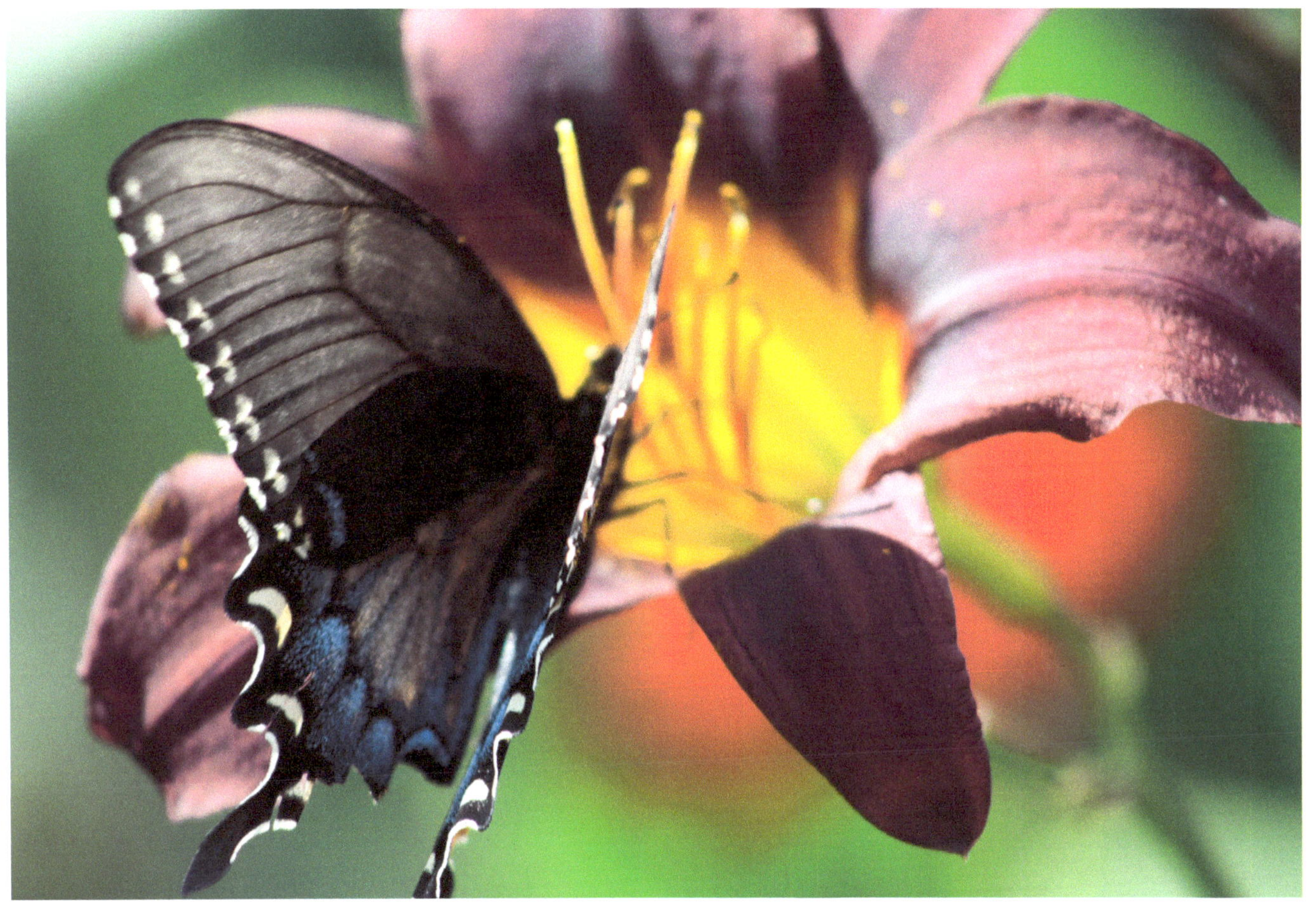

Sallow Tail Butterfly on a Day lilly

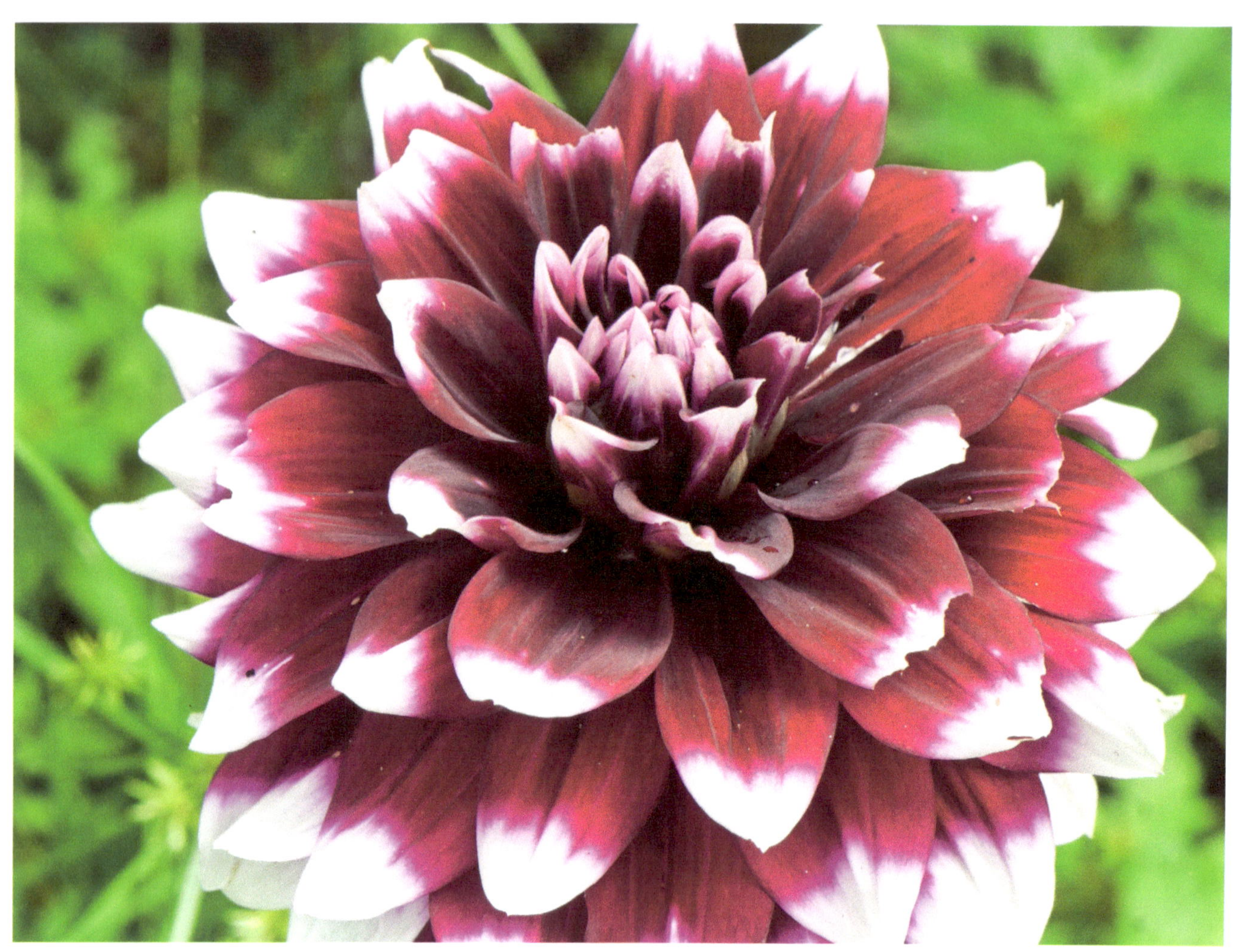

Dahlia

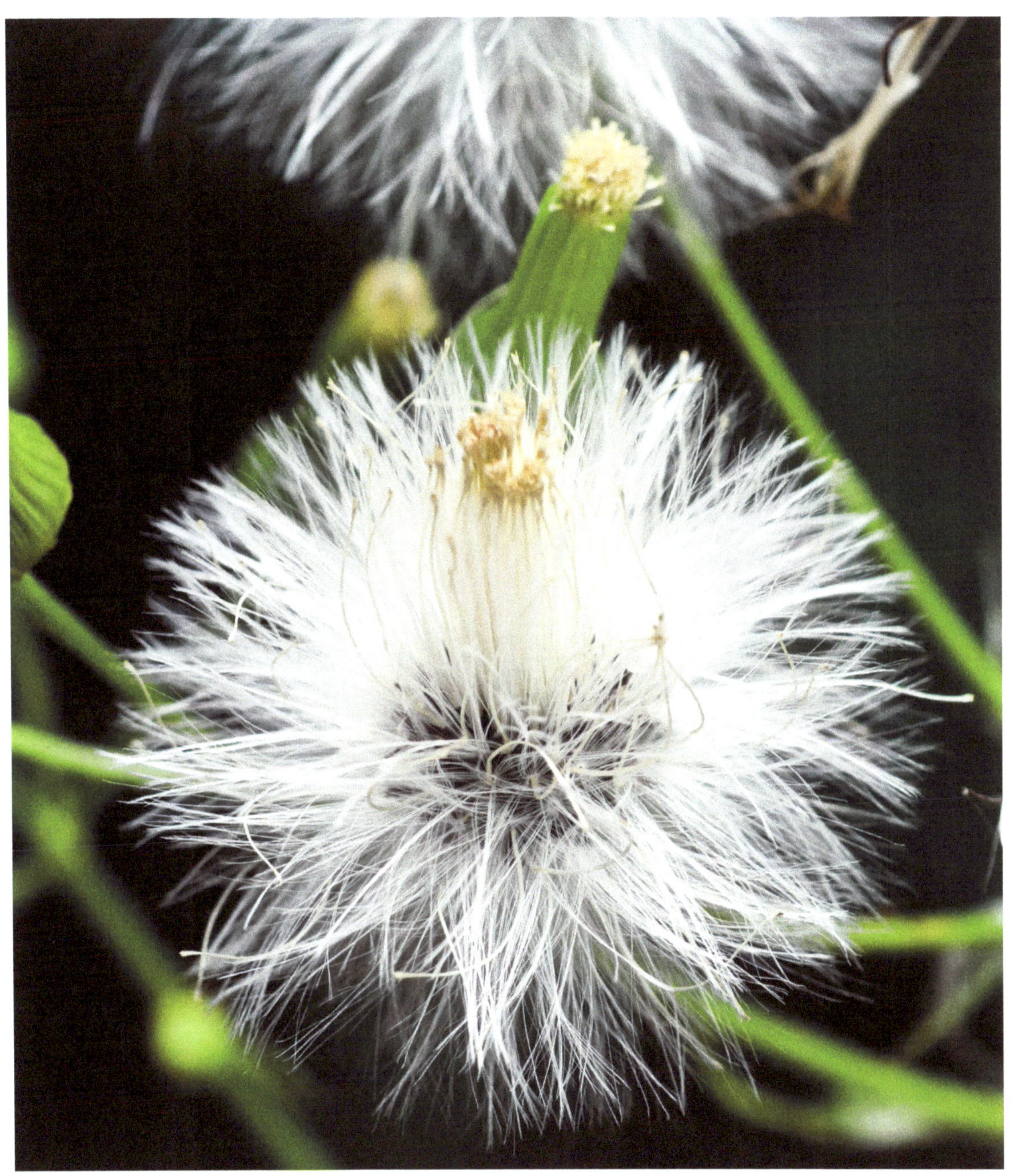

Confederate Jasmine Late Fall

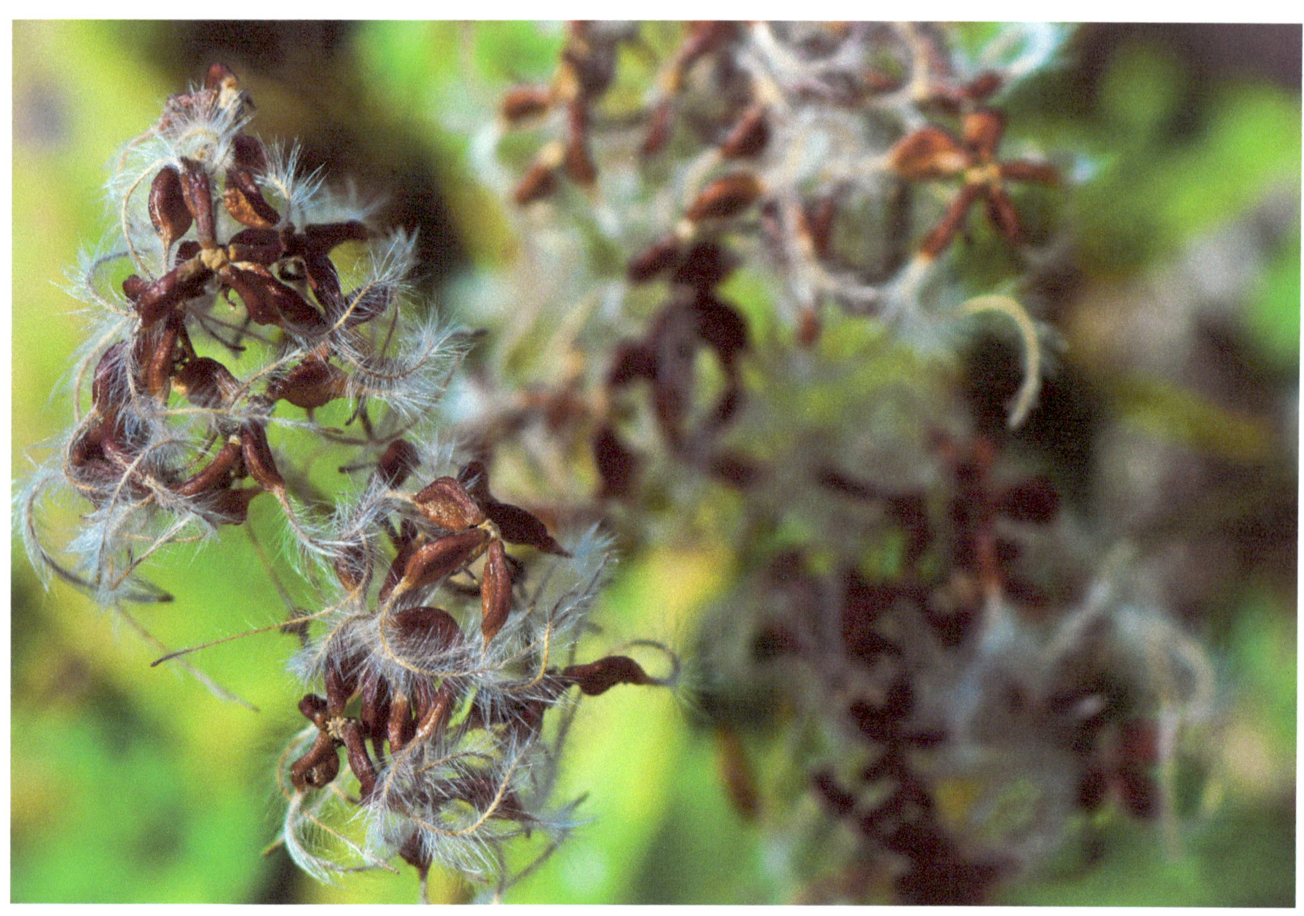

Confederate Jasmine   Early Winter

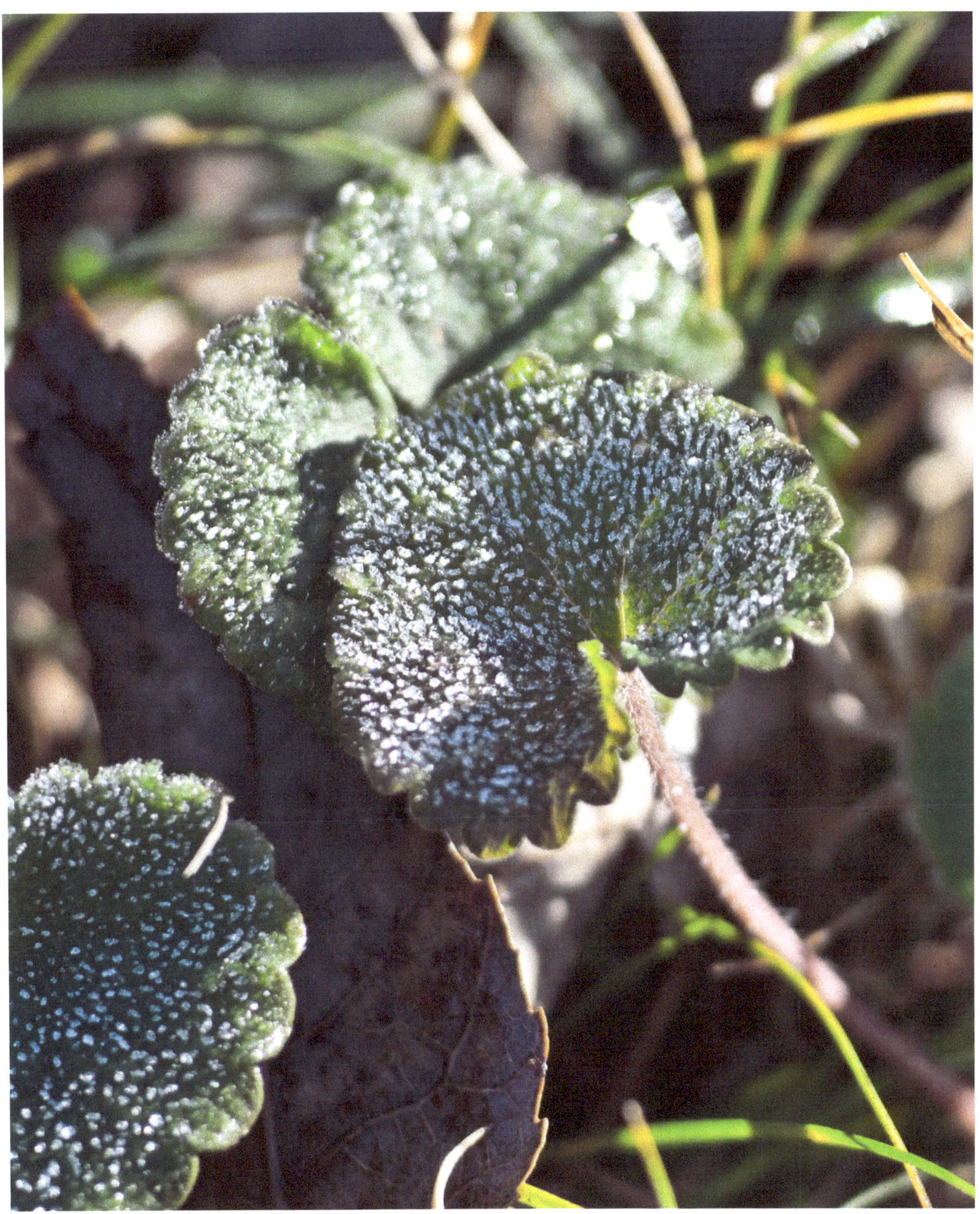

First Frost

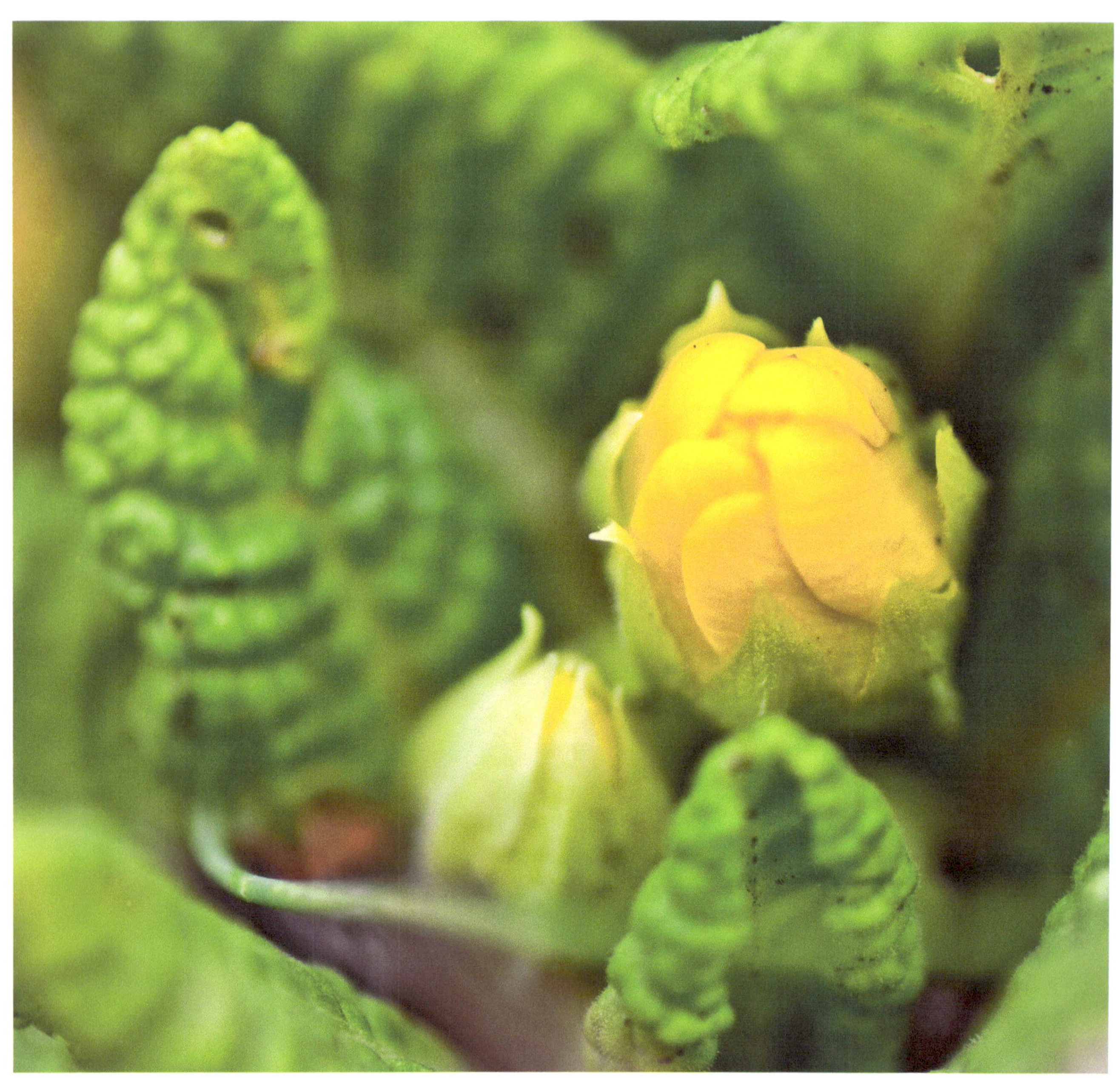

First Bloom Primrose

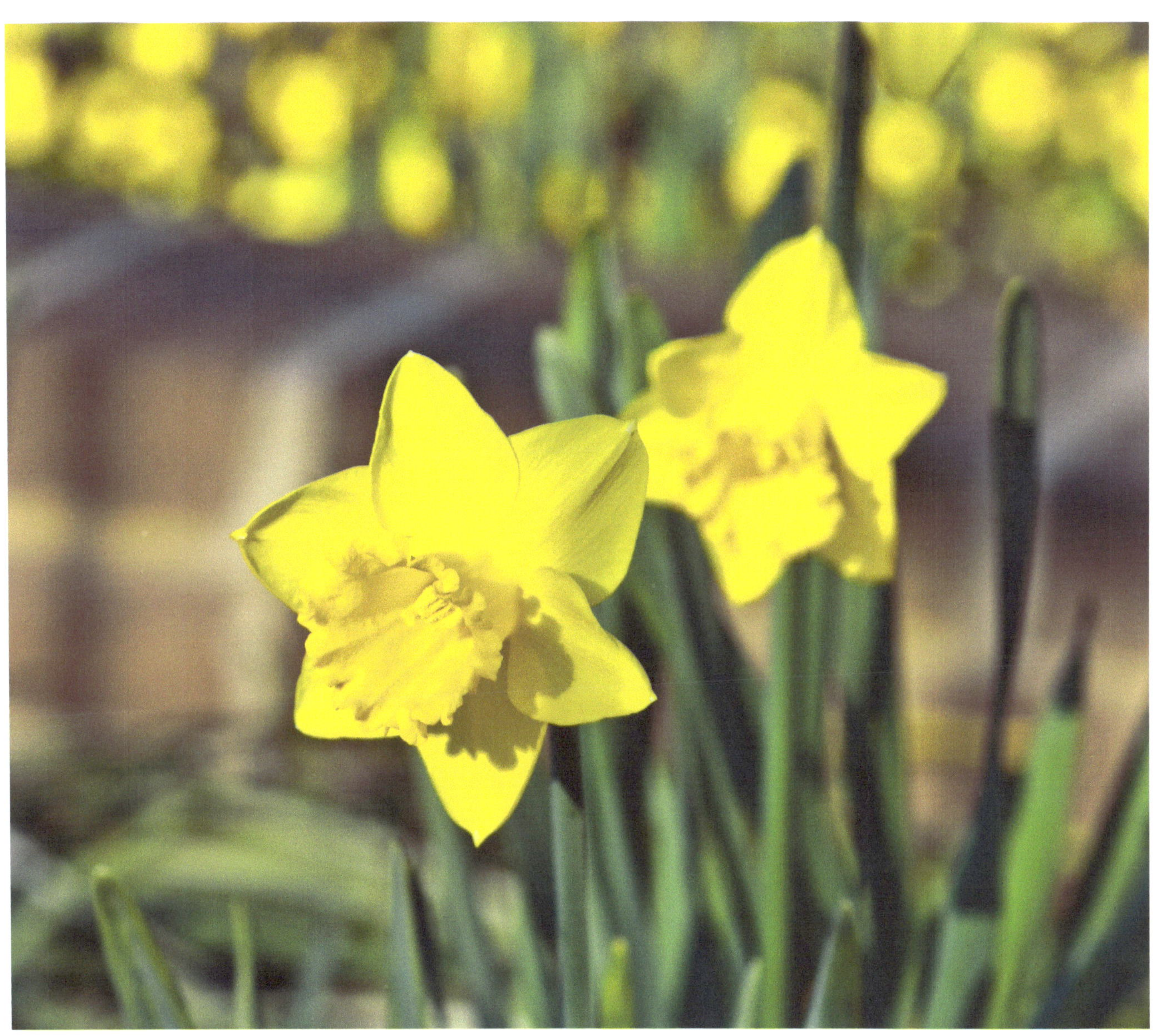

The Daffodils of Spring

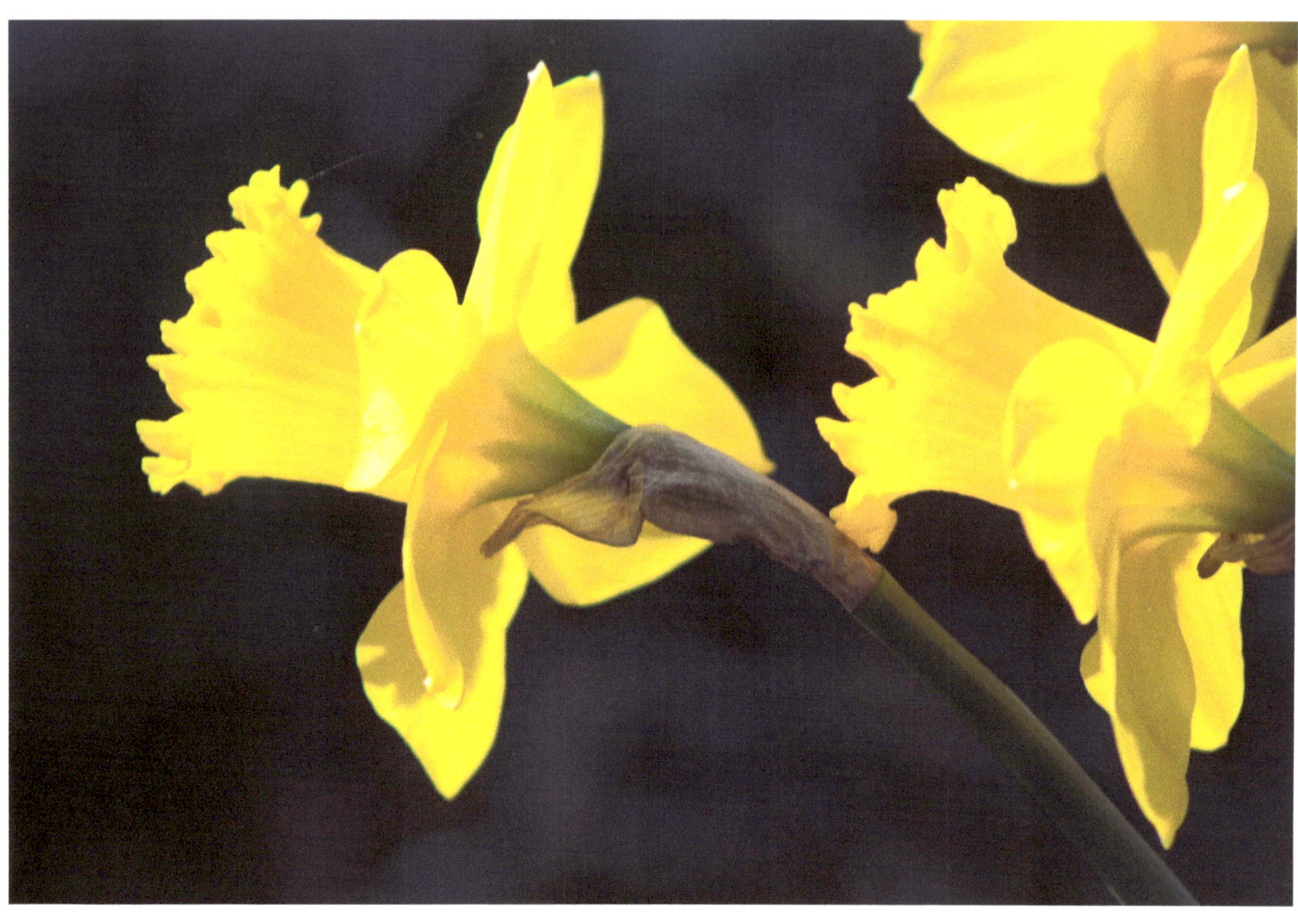

Bright yellow daffodil Close Up

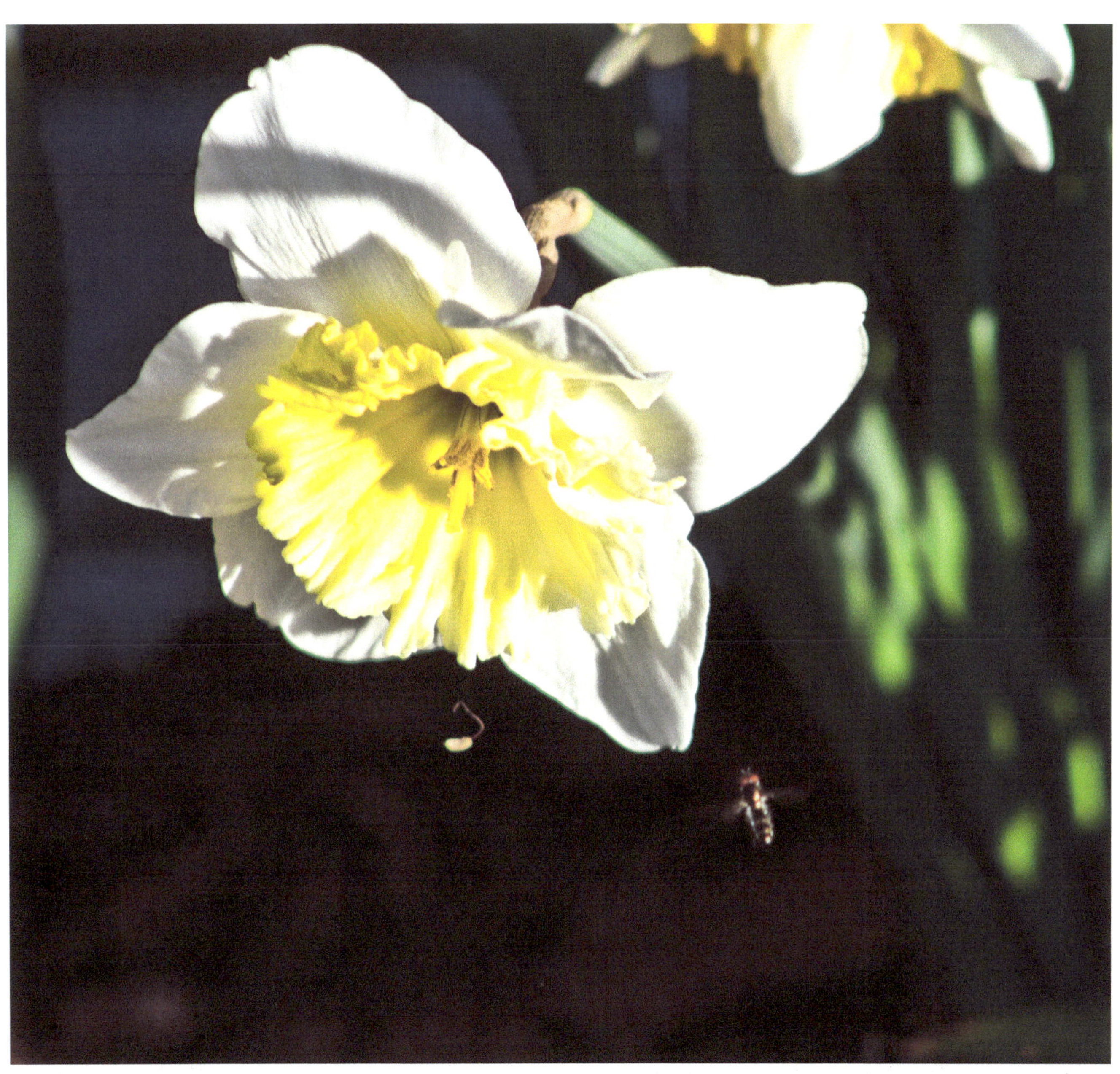

The Bee and the Daffodil

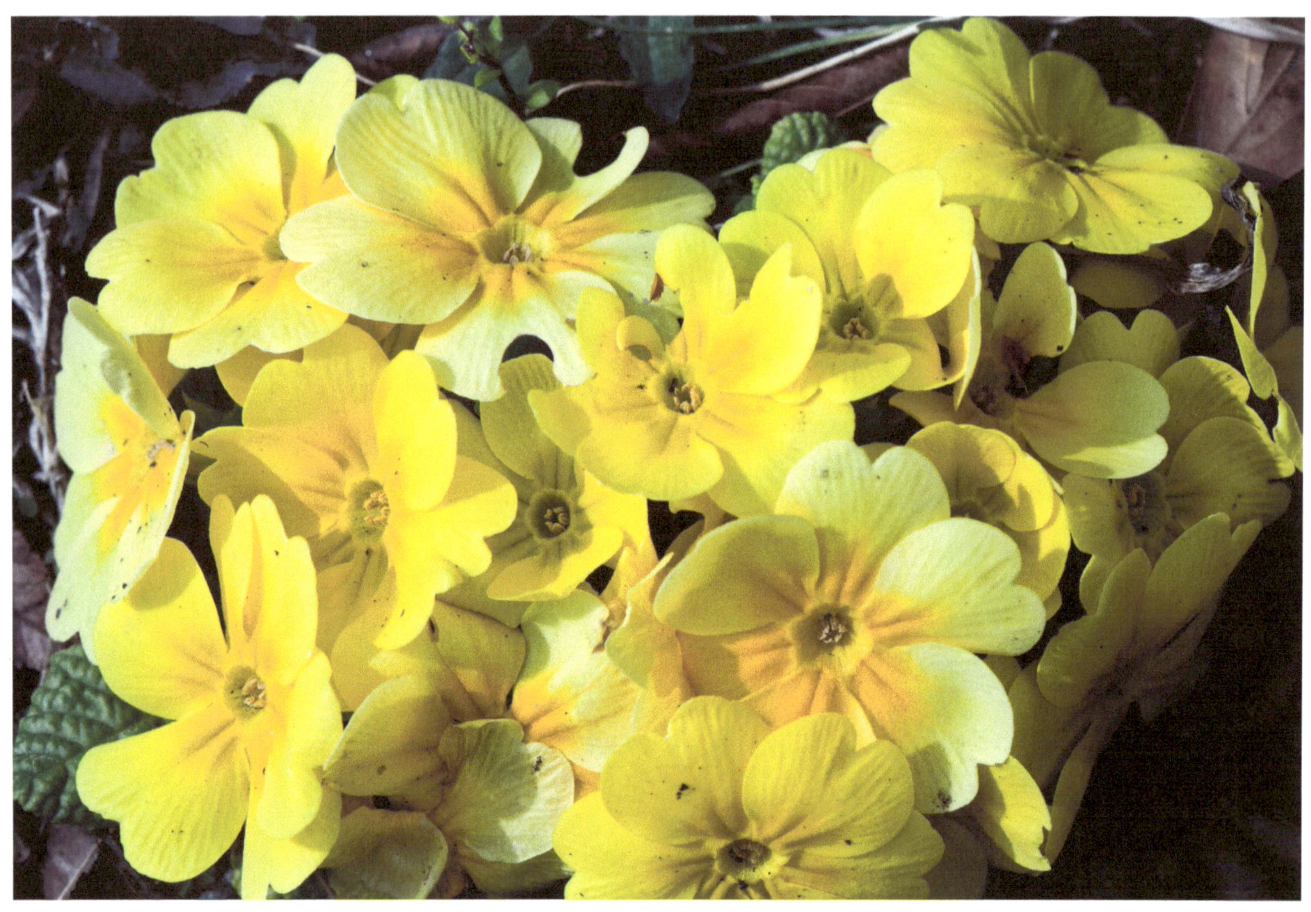

Primrose in Full Bloom

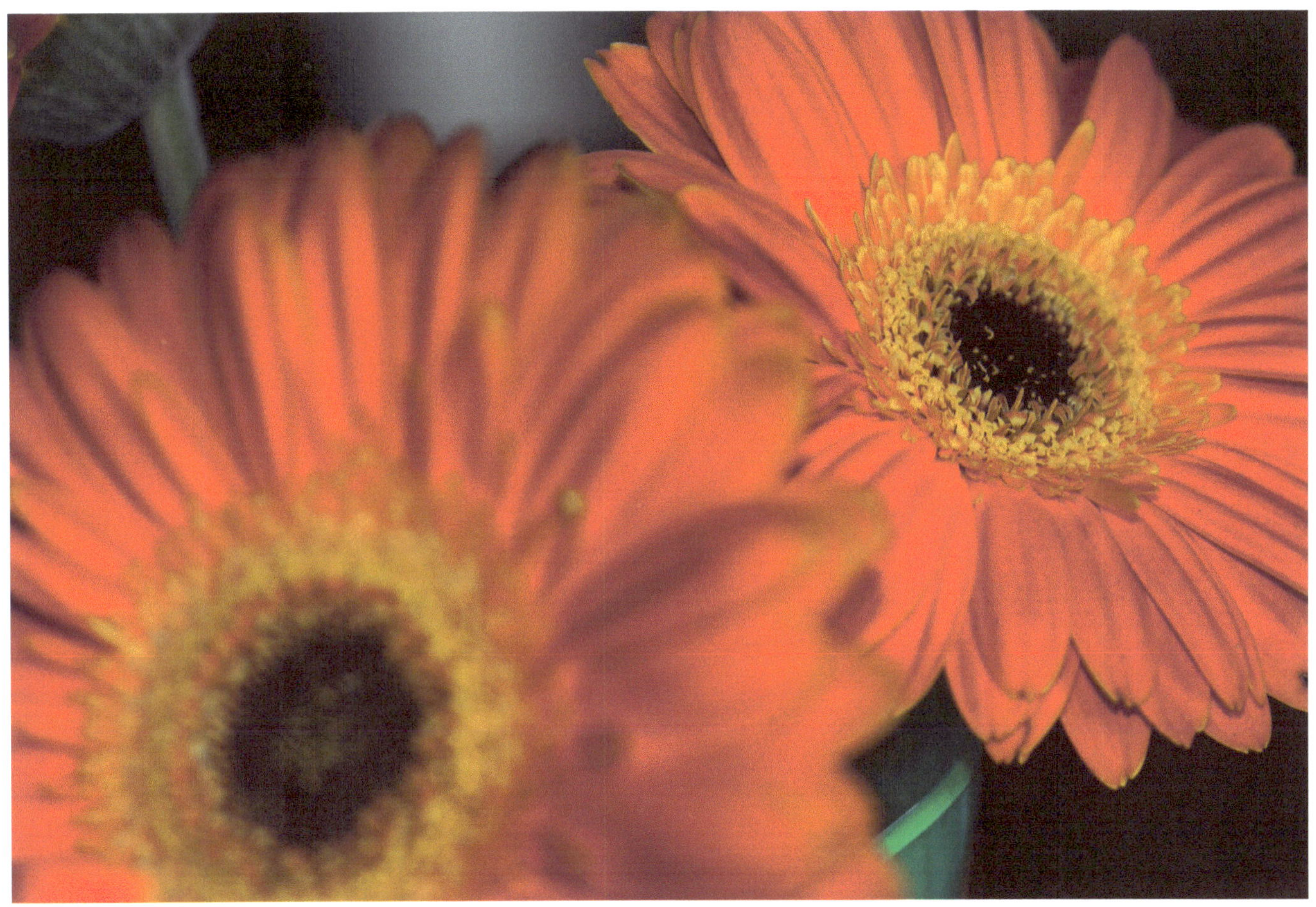

Orange Gebera Daisy

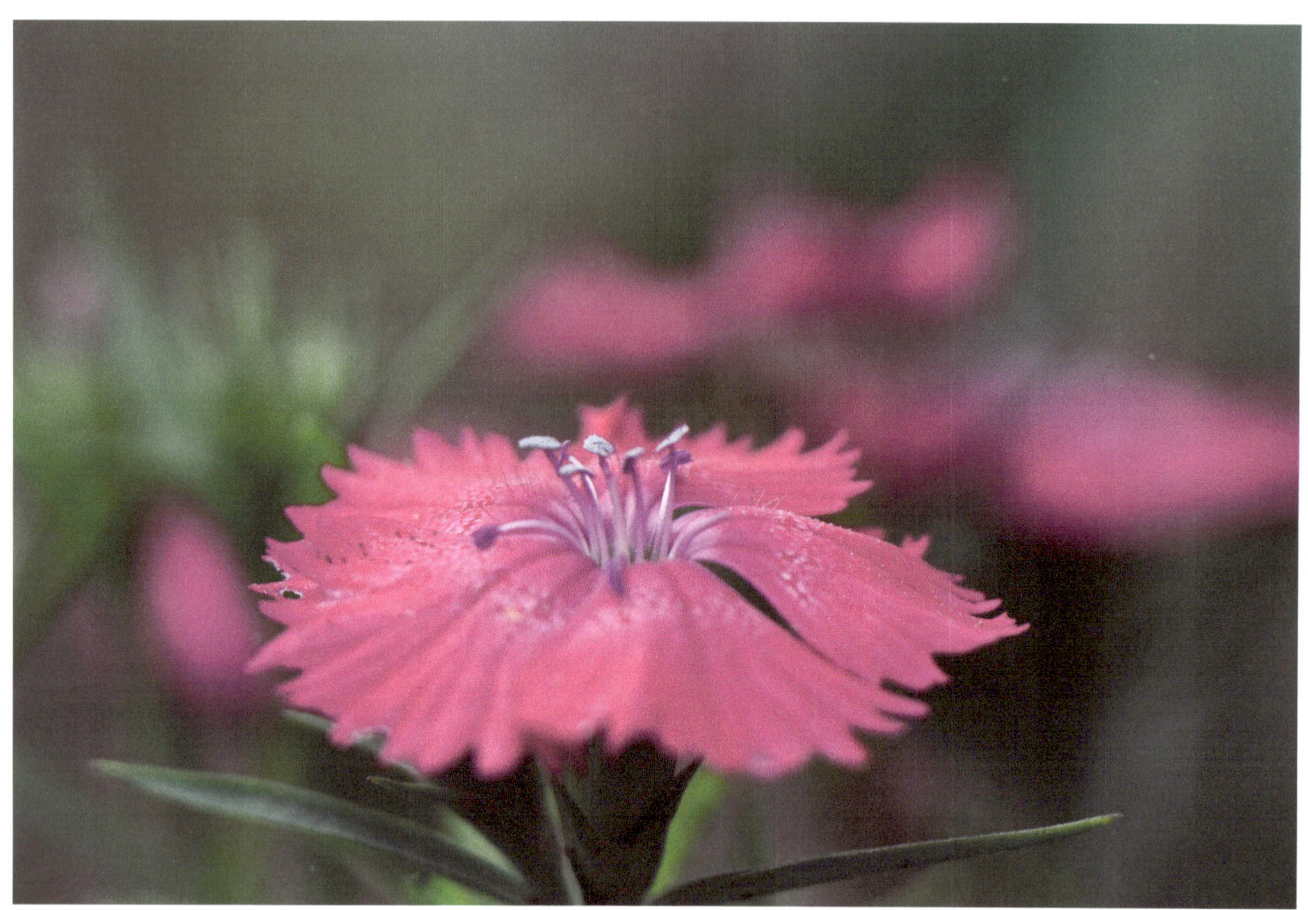

Hot Pink Dianthus Close Up

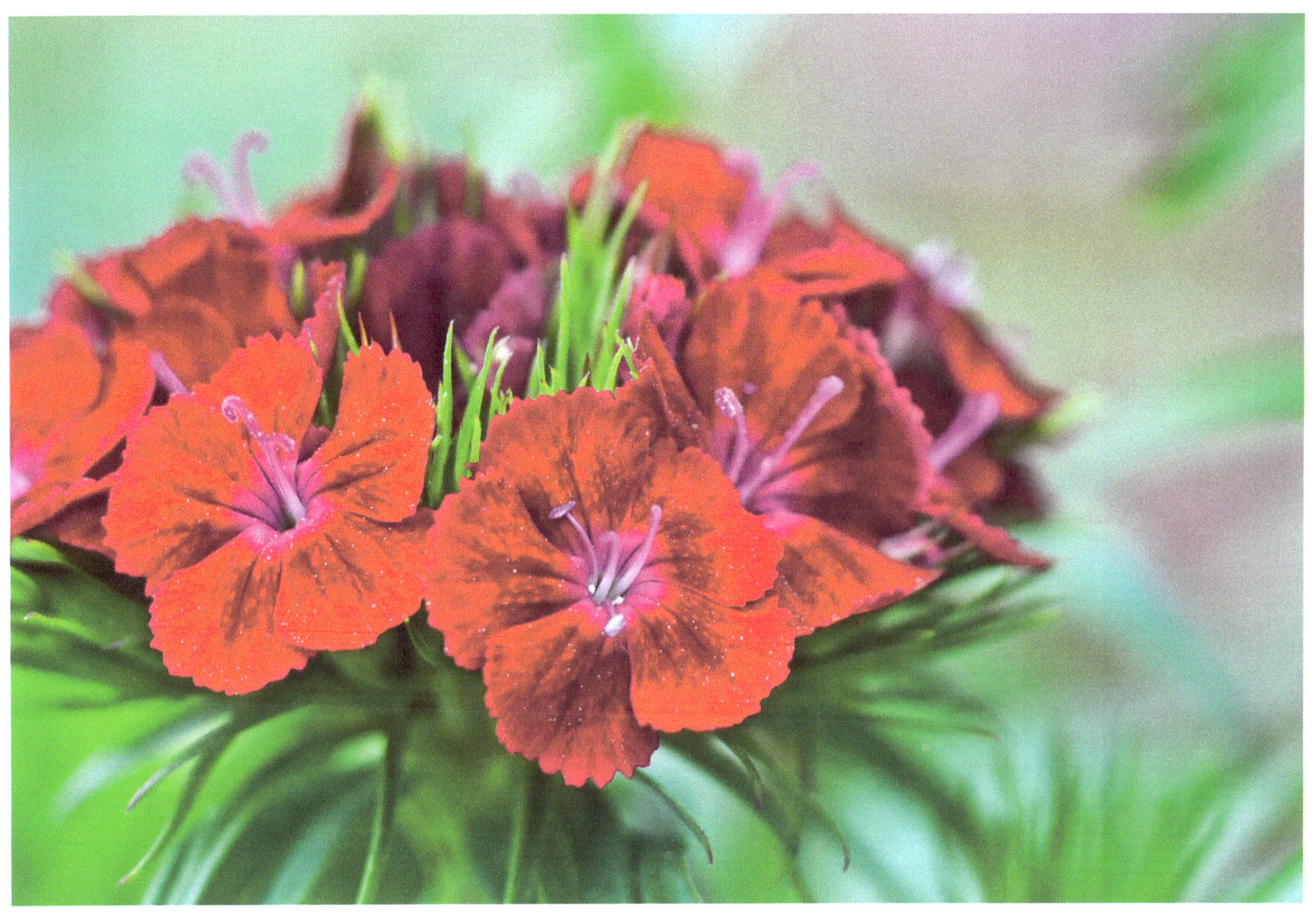

Red Sweet William

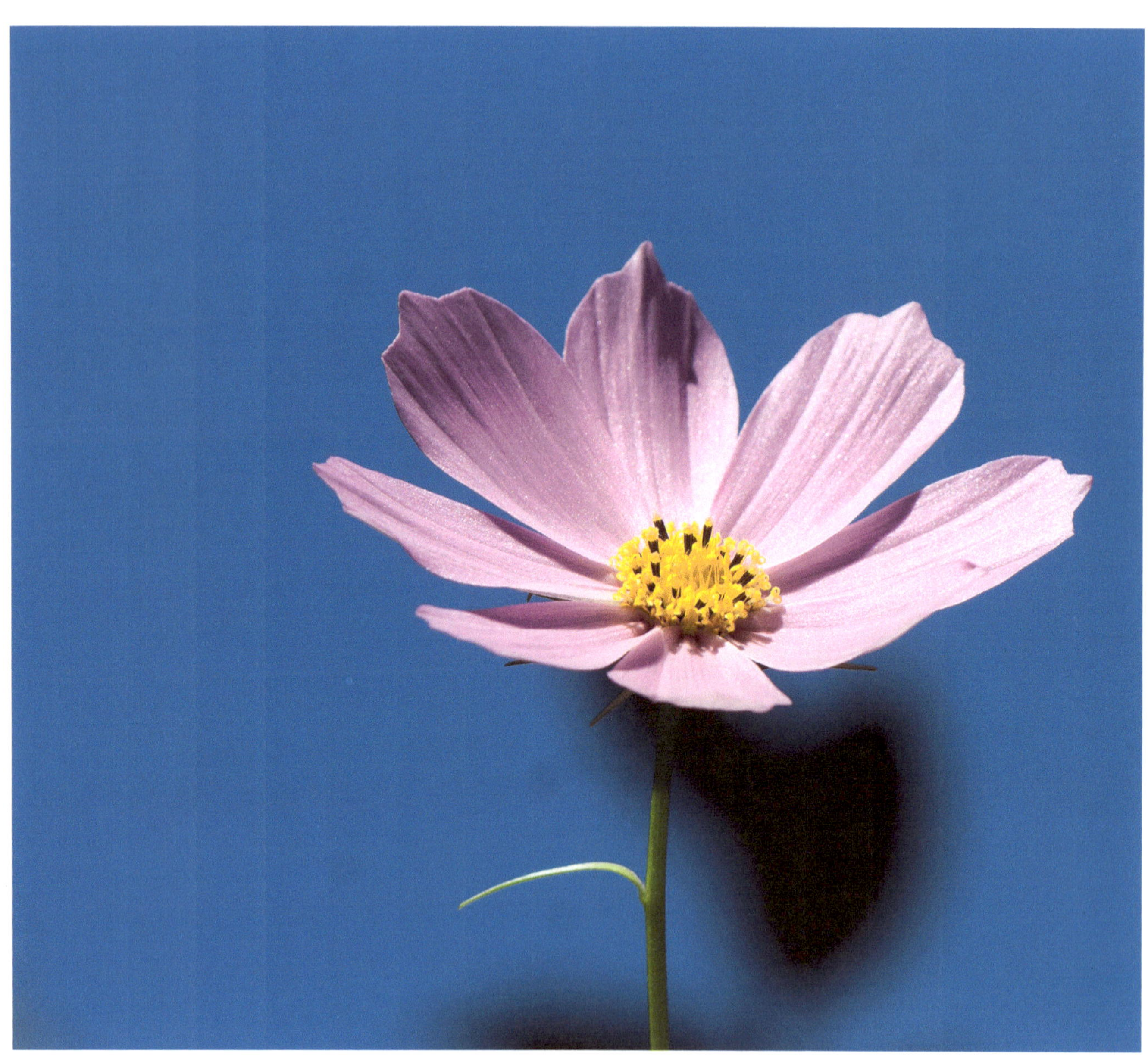

Lavender Cosmos

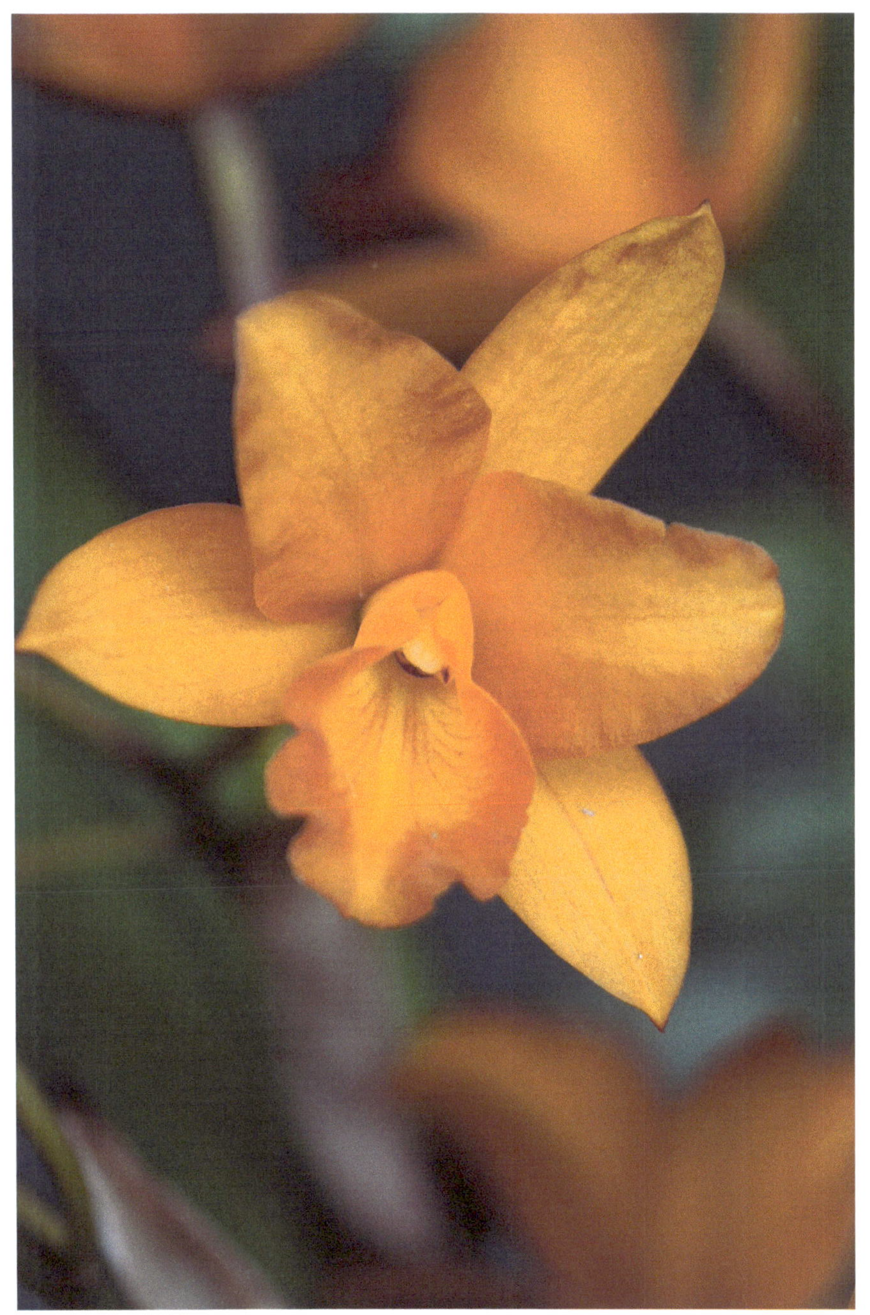

Orange Orchid

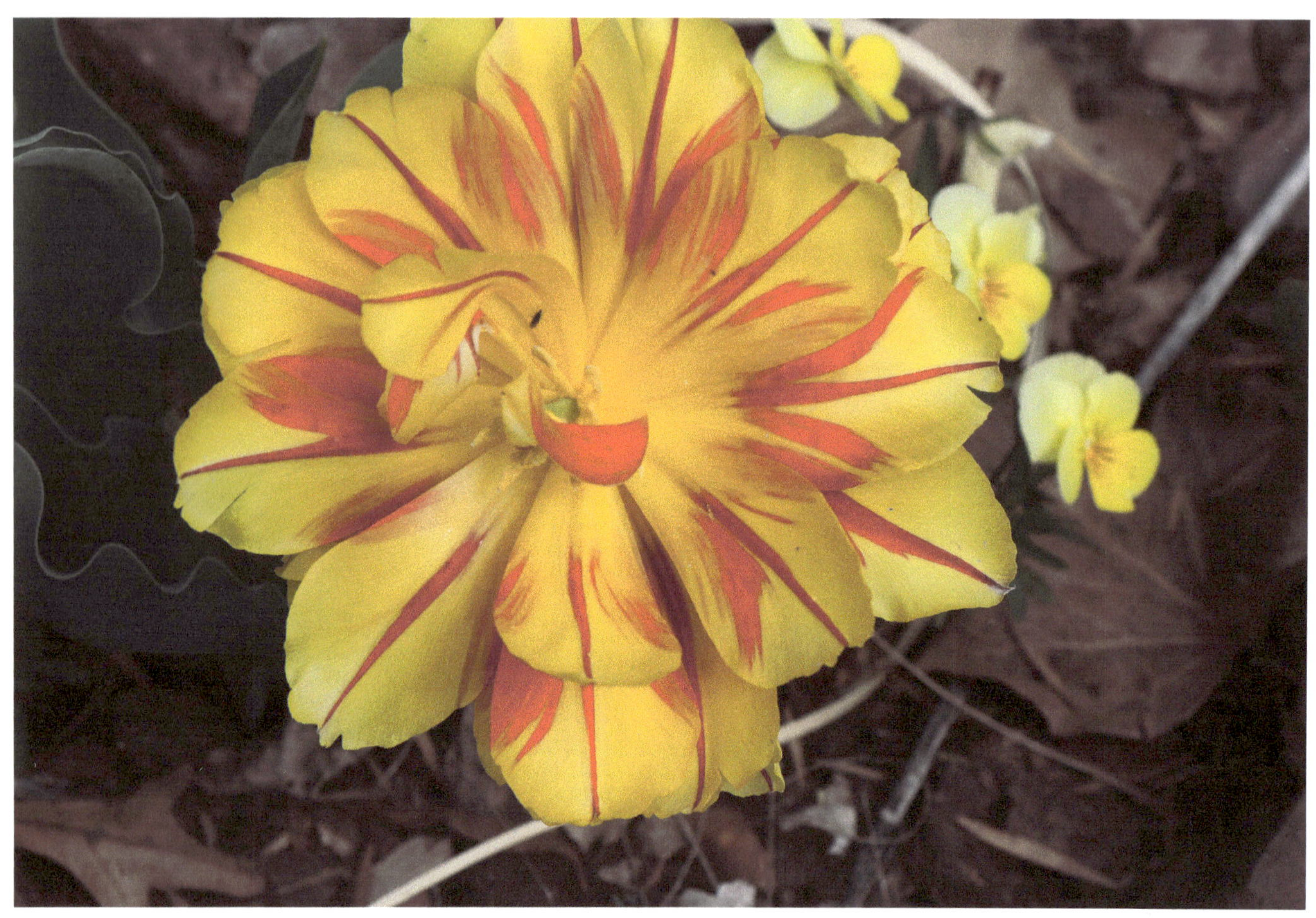

Yellow and Red Tulip

I hope that you have enjoyed flipping through the pages of this book. Please leave feedback. Thanks

Thomas Roth Jr.

Websites that might be of interest.

www.missingtoepublishing.webs.com

www.exit65thebook.webs.com

www.ingramcontent.com/pod-product-compliance
Lightning Source LLC
LaVergne TN
LVHW070155110826
845147LV00002B/404

* 9 7 8 0 6 1 5 8 2 1 9 1 7 *